Concepts in the Social Sciences

Series Editor: Frank Parkin

Published Titles

Concepts in the Social Sciences

Rights

Michael Freeden

Open University Press

Milton Keynes

Open University Press
Celtic Court
22 Ballmoor
Buckingham
MK18 1XW

First Published 1991

British Library Cataloguing in Publication Data

Freeden, Michael *1944–*
    Rights. – (Concepts in the social sciences).
    1. Rights
    I. Title.   II. Series
    323.4

    ISBN 0 335 15573 1
        0 335 15572 3 (pbk)

Typeset by Scarborough Typesetting Services
Printed in Great Britain by J. W. Arrowsmith Ltd., Bristol

For Daniella and Jonathan

Contents

Preface

Three themes run through this book. First, it examines briefly some of the major concerns of contemporary rights-theory. Second, in so doing it concentrates on the universe of theories and statements about rights in order to learn more generally about the modes and patterns of human thought-behaviour concerning politics. The concept of rights is particularly useful in this context because it straddles the notion of the individual and the notion of the political association, engaging with questions relating both to the private and to the public, and informing us about human aspirations and people's attitudes towards themselves both as political actors and as members of communities. Rights have manifest meanings known to their users as well as latent meanings which the student of rights has to uncover. The main emphasis of this book is on the ideological decoding of the role the concept of rights plays in political language rather than on the truth status of arguments about rights. Its aim is not to construct a theory of rights but to use the first order thinking-acts of people who do as the subject matter for second order analysis. That analysis is a central function of political theory. On the basis of that understanding (third) the case will be put for some underestimated interpretations of rights. These will not necessarily identify correct meanings but will rather regard them as plausible underpinnings to the developments in political thought and practice that typically accompany the emergence of civilized standards within modern welfare states. The emphasis throughout is on how rights *are*, *have been* and *can be*, not on how they *ought* to be, employed. Readers must feel free to use the following analysis as a basis for their own preferences.

I am grateful to Bill Jordan and Joseph Raz for their helpful observations on the typescript. Brian Barry and Robert Goodin assisted by commenting on earlier work of mine on rights, out of which this project developed. Irene, Daniella and Jonathan generously waived some of their rights, and took on supererogatory duties, in order to enable me to complete this book.

Michael Freeden
Mansfield College, Oxford

The Concept of Rights

Approaches and methods

The concept of rights has become one of the most reputable and positively connoted in political theory. The desirability of promoting in principle the ideas represented by the concept is far less controversial than, for example, the promotion of equality, democracy or even liberty.[1] Only a minority of viewpoints, such as the Marxist critique and some extreme versions of consequentialism, point to the possibility that adherence to rights might cause social or human damage. Modern political theory, which may be said to have begun with Hobbes, locates the notion of rights at the centre of its debates. The liberal state and constitutional theory have emphasized rights as fundamental building blocks of the social order, sometimes even as its *raison d'être*. The latter half of this century has witnessed a proliferation of concern about human rights in general as well as interest in the particular rights of categories of human beings (such as women, children, homosexuals, the elderly, the handicapped, the unborn and even future generations). Specific institutions have been established to promote human rights. Two hundred years after its revolution France erupted in a blaze of celebratory publications and events to commemorate what is now portrayed as the revolution's most enduring and fundamental legacy: *la déclaration des droits de l'homme et du citoyen*.[2] All this presents a challenge to the analyst of rights: why is 'a right' such an attractive term, what role does the concept play in political debate and in social organization, what does it signify to its diverse users, how does it obtain its range of meanings, and how, if at all, can that range be assessed?

In contradistinction to the method adopted by some philosophers I shall not attempt to construct an ideal system, or a conclusive list, of rights, nor will I endeavour to answer the question of whether human beings are intrinsically rights-bearing entities. I will also abstain from confronting the issue of whether rights exist independently of our knowing about them (if they did they would need to be discovered rather than invented). This reticence does not reflect any intellectual hesitation to take on these central issues but pertains to the particular nature of this inquiry. At its heart is a concern not with the retrieval of the logical and semantic relationships between, and the implications of, statements about rights, nor with their grammatical structure, nor with stipulated resolutions of ethico-philosophical issues,[3] nor even with exploring or delineating their unceasing intricacies,[4] but with analysing the general paradigms human beings employ when they think (as professionals or amateurs) about political issues. This is a book about human behaviour: the thought-behaviour of people when they reflect on rights. Its purpose is to elucidate the patterns of such thinking, to explore the combinations of ideas utilized in different theories and to understand why different implicit and explicit assumptions about rights lead to different political arrangements and solutions. It will do so, among other means, by uncovering the assumptions that have to hold in order for a particular theory to be deemed true or false. It will, of course, consider some of the main philosophical and legal approaches but only as part of the subject matter of this study, not in order to associate itself directly with those genres of scholarship. This book has no pretensions to be inclusive; its aim is rather to identify central issues and problems.

How do we go about understanding what a right is? The meaning of a concept is shaped by the range of further concepts that are attached to it and support it. Concepts as units of political theory do not occur in a vacuum. All too often analyses of rights pay little regard to the concrete and variegated ways in which the concept is underpinned by a host of related terms that act crucially to establish its different meanings.[5] The concept of a right is linked to concepts such as liberty, equality or individuality. Any actual usage of the word 'right' will be connected to specific meanings, plucked from a spectrum of possible meanings, of each of its adjacent concepts. The resulting configurations will enable the content and role of 'right' to be interpreted. The range of related concepts is very wide and I shall concentrate only on some of the most salient. For example, notions of human nature and social structure may be extrapolated from any given use of the concept of rights. These notions provide in turn particularly illuminating insights into the ideological positions that are embedded in seemingly impartial or universal theories.

Unless we postulate an essentialist view of concepts as bearing inherent meanings they are more usefully seen – as is the language of which they form a part – as products of a group or groups, who then consume them and transmit them further. On the social and political level some of those groups are composed of politicians, reformers, intellectuals, and secular and religious moralists. But rights are also the focus of interest of three major groups of scholars: historians of (political) ideas, lawyers and philosophers. These groups all approach the subject from a somewhat different perspective, although within each group there are substantial variations and profound disagreements. There are some notable overlaps, too – jurisprudence straddles law and philosophy – but on the whole these disciplines have established distinct traditions of analysis. A synthesis of their approaches is neither intellectually feasible nor culturally desirable. Nevertheless, it may be possible to identify common features and explain some divergences.

The work of philosophers on the subject of rights is, of course, highly valuable to students of social and political thought, despite some differences of perspective and emphasis. Recent philosophical debates in particular have produced helpful insights into the formal properties of rights, the relationships among people that rights imply and the actions or non-actions they entail, the distinction between liberties and claims, the links between rights and duties, the differences and similarities between forbearance-rights and welfare-rights, the bearing that the notion of a 'person' has on rights, and the connection between utilitarianism and rights-theory. Quite apart from the inherent worth of those exchanges to the pursuit of philosophical concerns, they greatly enrich our understanding of the roles rights play in the construction of political-belief systems and in the world-view of those who employ them. Occasionally, philosophical requirements are couched in terms too stringent to allow for the construction of a satisfactory case for human rights.[6] It is precisely at that point that an examination of the existing arguments for rights, however flawed, may lead us to different, possibly more useful, information about the subject.

Legal treatments of rights draw attention to some precepts that regulate relationships among people, enhance our comprehension of the civil context of rights, and direct us to interpret them within a system of authoritative and binding social rules. The most famous legal analysis of rights is that of Hohfeld, who divided them into four categories of relationships between right-bearer x and right-addressee y, and explained them by their corresponding correlatives.[7]

1 x has a liberty (or privilege) to do A – when x has no duty towards y not to do A, and y has a 'no-right' towards x. Singing in the bath is an example.
2 x claims A from y – and y has a duty towards x to do A: for instance, provide food or protection.
3 x has a power to bring about a certain consequence for y; an example would be a policeman requesting to see the licence of a speeding driver, who is thus under a liability.
4 x has immunity – when y lacks the authority to bring about a certain consequence for x and is thus under a disability. For instance, elderly people may be immune from being drafted into the army.

The scheme in general contributes precision to the examination of legal rights: the first two types of rights have become central to any rights-discussion and will reappear in the following pages; indeed all rights will exhibit one or more of the scheme's relational features.[8] But Hohfeld's categorization makes no attempt to clarify why people should be thought to have rights, or what the function of a right is.

Legal analyses also add detail to the range of specific rights that individuals may claim, employ 'more determinate modes of reasoning',[9] show how to protect rights by means of enforceable sanctions, and enable us to evaluate the legitimacy of the political systems and the efficacy of the social control and order that arise from the existence of civil, political and social rights. This is often related to feasibility and other general issues under the umbrella of legal positivism. Legal positivism locates the origin of rights in established rules, as in the following definition: 'to establish that A has a right . . . it is necessary to demonstrate that there is or is not a rule which warrants, entitles or enables A to have or do the thing or act in question, this warrant having specific legal consequences'.[10] This raises the possibility that rights could be seen as strident claims made by individuals insisting on the legal or formal justice due to them[11] rather than as an index of humane decency in a civilized society. Moreover, the existence of rules is no indication of whether the rules are right, of whether they establish reasonable and valuable entitlements or whether they entirely omit others. Both the philosophical and legal disciplines frequently eschew the historical and ideological contexts in which rights-discourse takes, and has taken, place. This is not to suggest that these latter contexts are more important, merely to assume that any intelligible discussion about rights in a society must appeal to all the above dimensions of analysis.

Theorists who restrict their analysis to positive rights abandon the analysis of moral or natural rights because they regard the latter as intuitive, non-determinable and metaphysical, hence unhelpful.[12] Although we may sympathize with such a position, it is not necessary to go along with it. People *do* assume that moral rights exist, and they behave accordingly. Consequently, we want to know what happens when they make such an assumption. In this way we circumvent the question of whether that assumption is a true or false one; we could, for instance, happily adopt the view that a belief is false and still devote analytical attention to the *fact* that the belief exists and discuss the impact of that fact on both theory and practice. Whether rights *exist*, or are figments of the human imagination, or are what lawyers call legal fictions, is thus analytically irrelevant.

Rights-theorists frequently address themselves to problems such as what beings can have rights; why human beings have them; what the grounds or bases are on which human beings can claim or be allocated rights; and what kinds of rights exist. These questions, irrespective of their philosophical profundity, interest the analyst of political thought primarily because the various ways in which they are answered provide fundamental clues to understanding how and why human beings think about politics the way they do. For many scholars that variety cannot *in principle* be overcome. It reflects the essential contestability of concepts, a view that holds that theoretical disagreements about the substance and meaning of concepts such as rights will always persist and can never be resolved into universally agreed responses.[13] Nor, indeed, have such unequivocal responses existed in historically demonstrable practice. But this hardly requires us to abandon rights-analysis. It requires instead that we shift the emphasis to three simple questions. What do people mean when they maintain that human beings have rights? What benefits, or costs, do users of language and the deliberate or inadvertent formulators of ideologies believe to accrue from rights-discourse? What can we learn about the political thought patterns of human beings, and the functions of those patterns, from the various ways they employ the language of rights?

A definition

The spectrum of definitions pertaining to a right is broad and illuminating in its different implications and ideological positions. For example, one approach sees rights as 'normative attributes' that belong to persons – the term philosophers use for self-conscious human beings, conceiving of themselves as initiators of purposive actions.[14] Another approach regards rights as entitlements to choose.[15] A third explains rights 'positively as entitlements to do, have, enjoy or have done'.[16] A fourth contends that rights 'always and necessarily concern human goods, that is, concern what it is, at least in normal circumstances, good for a person to have'.[17] Rights can be 'possessed, enjoyed, exercised' and 'claimed, demanded, asserted'.[18] We shall repeatedly encounter these views and others.

We must also take note of a significant distinction. To assert that human beings have rights is not identical to asserting that they have human rights. The latter complex term has developed this century into a key phrase, denoting a pre-eminent notion of rights. It would hardly include, for example, my right to use a pedestrian crossing without having to weave my way through moving traffic unless, perhaps, there were no other way of ensuring my mobility. For some theorists, human rights are a subset of rights in general;[19] but it is plausible to reverse this order, to say that human rights are the most basic, pertaining to what is essentially human, while other categories of rights are more specific, limited and, normally, derivative.

What kind of social activity and thought-behaviour do people engage in when claiming to have human rights? To claim to have a human right – the basic kind of right that will exercise us most in this book – is to employ a type of emphatic shorthand to indicate that some attributes or values ascribed to human beings are of overriding importance and may, or even should, be preferred over other attributes or values. Hence, *a human right is a conceptual device, expressed in linguistic form, that assigns priority to certain human or social attributes regarded as essential to the adequate functioning of a human being; that is intended to serve as a protective capsule for those attributes; and that appeals for deliberate action to ensure such protection.*

The interpretation of this definition may be assisted by eight further points.

1 It is impossible to answer precisely the question of who regards particular human attributes as essential. Because rights are an act of public language they cannot be solely the product of an individual's mind; they involve some acceptance by others. Societies contain significant – not necessarily majoritarian – groups that become acknowledged producers of dominant values, with moral, ideological or scientific appeal. These are then incorporated into intelligent public debate, although they are constantly subject to revision as knowledge and values change. Norms are thus established and claim rights-protection. Those producers may comprise a community with which the individual interacts or they may be prominent formulators of rights-theories who include that individual within the rights-bearing population irrespective of whether he or she is aware of that inclusion. Individual entitlement is inherently linked to what I shall refer to as *reasoned recognition* by others. Whether the rights in question *are* actually essential is a philosophical, biological or theological issue. Here they will be treated as carefully reasoned notions that reflect some mix of culture-relative and knowledge-impartial views of human nature.[20]

2 'Deliberate action' includes deliberate non-action, i.e. self-restraint, or forbearance, as a hidden form of managing action.

3 The action needed to protect the essential human or social attributes will have implications both for the rights-bearer and for those on whom the exercise of the right depends. If the attributes are human powers, such action may also involve enabling their expression or enhancement as long as that enablement is at least in principle considered feasible.[21]

4 Although many philosophers insist on the rational/logical derivation of a right from human attributes or from *a priori* moral
principles, an alternative view would ground a right not on
axiological or deontological foundations but on ideological or
conventional ones.[22] This suggests a difference between a right
and the notion of what is right. Righteousness is the opposite of
wrong and refers to what is correct, true or virtuous.[23] Although
we may have a right to what is 'right', no objective moral position
is necessarily implied by a right.

5 Rights-adherents usually aim to formalize or institutionalize
rights, primarily through law, though such social and political (as
distinct from moral or ideological) recognition and status are not
an essential precondition for claiming or identifying a right.
Another way of putting this is to regard the relationship between
rights and action as cemented through moral and/or legal
obligations.

6 Although the definition pertains to human rights, all rights may
protect desirable values, at least indirectly, and may be seen as
subsets of the general argument. My right to collect stamps,
although hardly essential to human flourishing, is a special case of
a general right to do anything not specifically forbidden for valid
reasons. That general right to free and unharmful action is usually
considered essential to human flourishing. Equally, the right to
have contract X respected does not signify the importance of X
but the crucialness that respect for contracts and promises has for
human and social functioning. These rights are derivative from
basic human rights.

7 Protection may be coercive and formal, or it may harness public
opinion in the form of an ethical imperative, or it may be
internalized through socialization processes. It may be graded
according to the nature of the protected attribute and it is
generally unlikely to offer watertight shielding.

8 A right ascribes a particular status or worth to the rights-bearer.
In their protective capacity for certain human (or group)
attributes rights signal the special importance of the entity
endowed with those attributes. Hence rights are more than the
reflection of duties towards passive individuals. They indicate not
only the particular importance of the duty, and of the interest or
ability safeguarded, but the special status of the rights-bearer.
They thus involve not merely a duty (of conduct) for the

right-upholder but an attitude of regard to the significant entities who are rights-bearers. This attitude is best not described as a duty at all; it is an ideological or ontological view of the social world. Because rights are value judgements expressing regard for human beings, they accord preference to conduct which embodies that regard over conduct which does not. (At this stage no ruling is proposed on the hierarchy or ordering of different rights.)[24]

When we say that human beings or groups have rights, we not only maintain (based on our imperfect empirical observations) that they have vital attributes that need to be expressed and safeguarded; we also affirm (metaphysically or morally) that they are unusually important objects and that the world we know would be inconceivable if their flourishing was not ensured and encouraged. In this way the normative sense of a right is incorporated into the analysis. This is not to suggest that a right can be logically deduced from moral foundations but that optimal human functioning is a practical, common-sense desideratum inasmuch as we want human beings to exist and to exist well. The needs and capacities protected by rights are humanly functional and necessary for the rights-bearer, rather than logically entailed by our understanding of what is objectively right.

Equally, the waiving of human rights is humanly destructive rather than logically impossible.[25] Their absence would deprive a community of rational goals, indeed of means of survival. We value the right to full expression and protection, provided it is not detrimental to individual and social well-being because, unsurprisingly, we particularly value a world in which human beings flourish. This avowedly anthropocentric view eschews any consideration of the objective 'goodness' of human existence. It may be grounded on the affinity most of us feel towards other human beings over and above other objects. It may also be grounded on some of the undoubtedly superior features of human beings or on the empirical fact that human beings alone seem to be able to control, adapt and modify their conduct according to rational criteria, as well as being capable of morality. If we were to abandon such anthropocentrism there would be no presumption in favour of honouring human rights any more than the rights of other living things.

We are also, of course, indicating the *equal* claim of every individual to bear rights – inasmuch as every individual needs to perform acts and express capacities – although individuals can claim to bear the *same* rights only in those aspects of their functioning that are identical to the functioning of others. This problem, which will be elaborated below, involves both the inequality of applying the same right to human beings with diverse attributes (e.g. the right to life, interpreted as the right to nourishment, will entail a different food intake for adults and babies), and the specific rights that certain categories may claim (e.g. mothers, the elderly).

Inasmuch as a right is an envelope concept it could be objected that its analysis cannot be detached from the phenomena it serves to protect – values, moral desiderata, needs, interests, human nature or welfare – and *their* conceptualization. The exclusive significance of a right as a concept could therefore be diminished. Up to a point that is correct. None the less, this need not entail abandoning an effective discussion of rights in favour of discussing those other concepts. Concepts are not necessarily clear-cut constructs nor can they be understood in a vacuum detached from the ideational configuration of which they are part. The point here is twofold. First, concepts obtain specificity and meaning by means of their relationship with adjacent and peripheral concepts that are in-variably attached to them. Without an appreciation of those intricacies of political argument a right would remain a vacuous notion. Second, although certain ideas and notions, such as claims, liberties, interests or duties, are analysable as distinct concepts, together they may form particular clusters associated with rights. Concepts need not be judged solely on the basis of their uniqueness, exclusiveness or logical coherence; they can also or alternatively be judged on the basis of their usefulness in ordering ideas, conveying knowledge and promoting comprehension.

I propose that the exclusiveness of the concept of rights lies not in *what* it protects – choice-capacities or welfare – but in its being simultaneously a *prioritizing*, *protective* and *action-demanding* concept. It is distinguished by a combination of these structural properties rather than by a specific content. Nor is it correct to suggest that 'institutionally, the important thing about human rights is that they are rights which have special protection'.[26] In the final analysis it is not rights that have special protection but the attributes they are designed to protect. Specifically, a right accords special status to an interest but it is not identical with it. This still leaves ample room for a detailed and sophisticated examination of the issues surrounding the protection of those valued interests, the particular status they obtain from being enshrined as a right, and the ordering and prioritizing functions exercised by the concept of rights. In other words, what happens to a value when it is elevated to the rank of a right and what are the consequences of that elevation for human behaviour and social organization?

A satisfactory theory of basic rights will have to pass at least three decisive tests. On a primarily philosophical dimension it will have to meet rational and logical standards; on a primarily ideological dimension it will have to be couched in terms that are emotionally and culturally attractive, as well as displaying the minima of rationality; and on a primarily legal dimension it will also have to be translatable into codes of enforceable action. One method of ensuring the last is to encode rights as civil and political rights. When we assert that human beings have rights – say, a right to life or to well-being – we simultaneously attempt to identify certain vital aspects of human essence and imply, as a corollary of that identification, the morally desirable or ideologically attractive requirement that people behave towards each other in such a way that those aspects may be preserved. This requirement is not logically entailed:[27] it is based upon our valuing – which is itself a concomitant of our being living and thinking creatures – not only the existence of human beings but their development, self-expression, mutual support and happiness and, to be even more specific, particular modes of such development, self-expression, mutual support and happiness. To argue otherwise would be to fudge the concrete ways in which rights-language and rights-arguments have developed over the centuries and are being expressed now; on another level, it would also fail to acknowledge that central areas of rights-discourse are open to inescapable ideological and philosophical dispute.

The Emergence of Rights in Political Thinking

Thomas Hobbes

A survey of some of the milestones of historical thinking on rights will assist us in identifying the key characteristics of the rights-debates whose chronological precedence has shaped subsequent arguments. Although the roots of the notion of rights may be found in late mediaeval European thought, and the natural-rights tradition already has its antecedents in the emergence of natural law in ancient Greek philosophy, it is customary to regard Hobbes as the starting point for the *modern* analysis of natural rights.[1] This is both correct and misleading. Hobbes developed what are now considered to be important components of the notion of rights, but he is not part of the humanist tradition that placed rights-discourse firmly within emerging liberal thought. His negative identification of liberties is akin, although not identical, to Hohfeld's concept of privileges because it lacks correlative no-rights of others,[2] and is by contemporary standards impoverished. On the understanding of rights suggested above – as a protective capsule for valuable human attributes – Hobbes's notion of a right is idiosyncratic and, on the surface, divergent.

> The Right of Nature [writes Hobbes] . . . is the Liberty each man hath, to use his own power, as he will himself, for the preservation of his own Nature; that is to say, of his own Life; and consequently, of doing any thing, which in his own Judgment, and Reason, hee shall conceive to be the aptest means thereunto.

Hobbes then goes on to specify: 'By Liberty, is understood, according to the proper signification of the word, the absence of externall Impediments' and 'Right, consisteth in Liberty to do, or to forbeare'.[3]

A number of interesting features are immediately noticeable. First, a right is related to *one* particular end – self-preservation – which is presented as an element of (independent) value, although only for psychological and behavioural reasons. Second, the right of nature is attached to individuals, who are the sole judges of the means to attaining the end it preserves. Third, it is within a person's right to pursue *anything* conducive to self-preservation – therefore a right is unlimited ('there is nothing to which every man had not Right by Nature')[4] and inconsiderate of other individuals; further, there is no independent criterion for assessing the relative value of rights-oriented actions when they conflict with each other. Hobbes regarded a right as pertaining to the unlimited exercise of will, not to the rational exercise of will for generally valued purposes. This is because a right is merely the absence of a duty – i.e. a liberty – and in a state (of nature) where duties are totally absent rights expand by default to become all embracing.

Fourth, if a right is a liberty, and a liberty signifies the absence of impediments, then a right denotes a condition, namely that of being able to use one's power. It is a descriptive rather than a normative term. Fifth, if a person can either choose to exercise that liberty or to forbear, then a right may be waived: 'Right is layd aside, either by simply Renouncing it; or by Transferring it to another.'[5] Strictly speaking, the right of nature consists of two facets, the one inalienable, the other not. In the first category, 'there be some Rights, which no man can be understood by any words, or other signs, to have abandoned, or transferred' – and this relates to the right to self-preservation. In the second category there exists the 'Right of Governing my selfe', and this may be ceded, together with everyone else's right to the same, to the sovereign.[6]

Although he used traditional terminology Hobbes detached the concept of natural right from that of natural law: 'Law, and Right, differ as much, as Obligation, and Liberty; which in one and the same matter are inconsistent.' All this weakens considerably the idea that rights preserve something important or worth preserving or, rather, limits the evaluation of that importance to private decisions and precludes the idea that a right is a guide to morally desirable action. As Finnis has observed, Hobbes 'deprives the notion of rights of virtually all its normative significance'.[7] Indeed, the obligation which for many modern theorists is the obverse of a claim-right is, for Hobbes, consequent upon the *abandonment* (or transferring) of a natural right and the ensuing contraction of the sphere of individual action. By renouncing or transferring my right I acquire a duty towards others not to hinder them in *their* exercise of the very right I have forgone.[8]

Clearly, Hobbes's conception of rights is predicated on further assumptions about human nature and the quintessence of human relationships. On closer inspection, in fact, his analysis of rights does not diverge from our definition of the concept. Rights do serve as a protective capsule for Hobbes's particular conceptions of human nature and social structure. Human nature revolves round prudential calculations necessary for the conservation of life, and round the passions, dominated by the fear of death. The right of self-preservation is simply the embodiment of this unbounded egocentric drive for survival, as the only, minimalist, valuable aspect of being human. It is, furthermore, linked to an asocial view of human organization which firmly locates the source of that value in individuals themselves, there being no alternative fulcrum from which to assess the good and the desirable and there being no external basis for the value of life itself.[9]

Finally, the protective capsule is paradoxically both as strong and as weak as its wielders can, or care to, make it. Connected as it is to the power of the right-bearer, it may be quite immune from infringements (which, in Hobbes's usage, cannot be distinguished from violations)[10] or pitifully exposed to them. Hobbes's view lacks the demands on the actions of others that are incorporated into a modern notion of rights, and which sustain their defensibility. It is precisely this indeterminacy of the strength of the capsule, with the ensuing insecurity and unpredictability, that causes rights-wielders to prefer a different arrangement and to put their pens to the dotted line of contract.

John Locke

In many ways Locke's account of rights is more traditional than Hobbes's, yet it has been more directly linked to modern liberal theory. Its traditionalism lies in its view of natural law as God's design for man. Hence man's duty to God is to realize that purpose and both scripture and reason can guide him on that path. However, Locke's more generous identification of fundamental human traits and needs[11] entails a more extensive specification of rights. Not only did he detect in people a sociability that Hobbes denied, but he asserted that in the state of nature all men were equally rational, capable of action and creativity, thus challenging the prevailing doctrine of the divine right of kings. That capacity for free action allows for human choice, although rational choice will not deviate from the morality of God's law. Within that sphere the laws of nature that pertain to human beings relate to the rationality of self-preservation and of preserving mankind in general,[12] liberally interpreted to include 'life, liberty, health, limb or goods of another'.[13] What is on one dimension a duty to God becomes on another a right against other men.

Thus, unlike Hobbes, Locke regarded natural rights as derivative from natural law. The law of nature and of reason directs 'a free and intelligent Agent to his proper Interest' – his general good.[14] The preservation of important human attributes and requirements are natural rights, to which another must be added: a natural quasi-political right to punish offenders against the law of nature. This derivative right is the basis for political society and can be forgone when a better method of defending man's rational capacities is devised – one offered by political society.

In sum, because men, and societies of men, have a moral duty of self-preservation, they 'will always have a right to preserve what they have not a Power to part with' – i.e. the right to life, to exist. And because 'we are born free, as we are born rational', human beings have an equal right to liberty and to sovereignty. Finally, 'Men, being once born, have a right to their preservation, and consequently to Meat and Drink, and such other things, as Nature affords for their subsistence.'[15] Locke extended the notion of property to include the ownership of one's life and sovereignty over one's actions as well as the possession of goods. These three natural rights correspond to the moral duties men bear to God; they are inalienable precisely because they are such duties.

Whether or not Locke provided a justification for capitalist property relationships, in which the inclusive right to common property is converted by individual labour into an exclusive one, is a matter of some debate.[16] Furthermore, although Locke's employment of

rights-language suggests on the whole a negative notion of forbearance towards the rights of others, there is a strong case for
contending that the right to freedom encompasses also the duty to
develop one's rationality.[17] What is not in question is the pre-
eminent liberal tone pervading Locke's treatment of rights when he
portrays them as accounting for and shaping the establishment of
political society. The function of government is the protection of
natural rights: the security and enjoyment of men's properties.[18]
The control of individuals of equal standing over their rights is the
basis for a consent (or social contract) theory of government,
whereas what rights protect and enable is important enough to
justify a restricted notion of political power as a trusteeship for the
safety and good of the people. The modern conception of rights as
moral constraints on governmental action which require institutional realization owes much to Locke.

Edmund Burke

The promulgation of the French Declaration of Rights of 1789 gave
an immense impetus to the debate about the rights of man. Three
different kinds of reaction are epitomized in Edmund Burke,
Thomas Paine and Jeremy Bentham. Burke's challenge to the
Declaration, which reasserted natural rights in the Lockian tradition, was a conservative one which did not dispute that rights
existed but disputed the *basis* of that existence. Slowly changing
conservatism has kept the essentials of his contentions in circulation
(although outside the mainstream of rights-theory) to this very day.
Above all, Burke attacked the abstract, metaphysical and simplistic
character of natural rights which he contrasted with the real rights of
men, which related to their particular history and complex circumstances, such as the rights and liberties of Englishmen. Those real
rights were prescriptive, 'an *entailed inheritance* derived to us from
our forefathers . . . without any reference whatever to any other
more general or prior right'.[19] Their reality was the result of
establishing the true nature of people in their social, national and
historical contexts.

   While professing not to deny natural rights, Burke was adamant –
in contradistinction to the Lockian tradition – that they could not be
translated into civil and political rights. Although some modern
progressive rights-theorists would not object to Burke's describing

civil and political rights as the 'offspring of convention' rather than innate, they would dispute Burke's employment of 'convention' as the accumulated wisdom of the ages which could not be challenged by the present exercise of individual, rational and equal wills. Burke reduced reason to the virtue of prudence and elevated prejudice – the feelings people have about their historical institutions – in its place. His intention was to depict government as a convenience that would restrain the members of a society, satisfy their wants and ensure the upholding of a natural hierarchical social order in which the notion of natural rights was 'morally and politically false'. Burke was adept at using the current language of radicalism while endowing it with traditional content. His interpretation of the social contract as an organic partnership between the dead, the living and those yet to be born is redolent of a strong sense of community; but it is a community that overrides and replaces the wills of individuals, locating their rights within a concrete society with established laws.[20]

Thomas Paine

Paine's *Rights of Man*, Part One, provided an immediate rebuttal of Burke's views. It echoed many Lockian premises which had themselves found expression in eighteenth-century Declarations and Bills of Rights. Rejecting the argument from history because it could go back to creation itself, Paine saw the origin of rights as divine. Man, having been created equal and rational, had natural – and *contra* Burke, imprescriptible – rights which were 'those which appertain to man in right of his existence'. Consequently, each generation had the right to make rational decisions for itself – the source of popular sovereignty. Man's natural rights included the Lockian rights to liberty, property and security, as well as the derivative right of resistance to oppression. But they also comprised 'all the intellectual rights, or rights of the mind, and also all those rights of acting as an individual for his own comfort and happiness, which are not injurious to the natural rights of others'.[21] These latter natural rights were retained as such in society, but the others – which individuals could not effect themselves – were converted into civil rights.

The novelty of Paine's view lay in extending natural rights to embrace, however tentatively, an early version of welfare-rights.

Despite a predominantly minimalist view of government, he allowed for some redistribution of wealth to those who had lost the fruits of their labour – i.e. their natural right to property – through unjust property arrangements. In the main, though, Paine's contribution to the natural-rights tradition was not as an innovator but as a popularizer who made the tradition accessible.[22]

Jeremy Bentham

From a very different viewpoint Bentham launched a famous attack on the concept of natural and imprescriptible rights as 'rhetorical nonsense, – nonsense upon stilts'. His critique of the French Declaration of Rights of 1791, on grounds of logic as well as substance, was devastating and systematic. The quasi-empirical language of 'flat assertion' that people had rights was peremptorily dismissed: 'reasons for wishing there were such things as rights, are not rights'.[23] Rights did not exist outside government; they could not be absolute without gross contradiction; their imprescriptibility appeared to remove them entirely from the sphere of law, and thus human direction, for the purpose of reform; their subjects (as in the case of property) and upholders (as in the case of liberty) were unspecified; they were based on an unsustainable belief in human equality. In sum, no Declaration of Rights, 'under any such name, or with any such design, should have been attempted'. We shall return to an assessment of some of these arguments. Undoubtedly, though, Bentham was intent on showing up natural rights as a *reductio ad absurdum*, and he accomplished that through rigorously literal and inflexible reading of texts, ignoring the fact that rhetorical nonsense can frequently make ideological sense.

Bentham was certainly making an important point when he called rights fictions. He went on to differentiate between the bad fiction of natural rights and the good fiction of legal rights, the latter fiction being necessary for human discourse.[24] As a legal positivist Bentham regarded law as a rational human contrivance necessary for social and political life. Rights could only exist within that framework and were not anterior to law: '*Right*, the substantive *right*, is the child of law: from *real* laws come *real* rights, but from *imaginary* laws, from laws of nature . . . come *imaginary* rights.'[25] Hence rights and legal duties were normally correlative.[26]

Specifically, Bentham distinguished between liberty-rights and rights to services, the latter subdivided into forbearance services and active ones, yet another early opening to welfare-rights.[27]

Most interestingly, Bentham subscribed to what was later termed the benefit theory of rights. A system of law was one of formal and coercive obligations. A right-bearer was simply a beneficiary of such an obligation; a right was the legal expectation of the discharge of a legal duty, intended to benefit the bearer.[28] A right was thus the obverse of a legal duty and it gave its bearer a power over the potential benefactor. A major feature of this legal approach was Bentham's insistence on the determinate and intelligible meaning of a right.[29] That precision of definition with its simplicity of promulgation is an advantage a legal right has over natural, human or moral rights though, as we shall see, often at the cost of generality, force and radicalism.

Finally, Bentham's significance lay in his being a principal architect of a powerful and still central philosophical doctrine – utilitarianism. On the surface there seems to be only one way of reconciling rights with his central principle of maximizing pleasure and minimizing pain: if rights are conducive to that end, they should be retained; if not, they should be superseded. That subservient status of rights is inimical to rights-centred theories and to the definition employed in Chapter 1. In fact, Bentham was ill at ease with the application of utility to *natural* rights: 'I know of no natural rights except what are created by general utility: and even in that sense it were much better the word were never heard of.' On the other hand, legal rights were subject to the test of utility: the degree to which they contributed to the happiness of a community.[30]

Like most Western political thinkers Bentham believed in the rationality of his political theory. But his concept of rationality was harnessed neither to the innate reason of the natural law tradition nor to the prudence invested in Burke's historical prejudice, but to the calculating and scientific aspirations of his notion of utility. It was also a conception remote from later human-rights thinking in its ahistorical and static approach to human nature. The test of Benthamite utility was one of the moment, accepting individual wants and desires at their face value and ignoring the developmental character of human beings. These defects were partially offset by a later transformation in utilitarian thinking.[31]

Thomas Hill Green

Green's importance lies in his input into modern liberal thinking about rights. He adapted nineteenth-century Idealist thought to British liberal concerns, and employed the concept of rights in a pivotal position. His treatment of the subject is interestingly representative of many modern philosophical analyses in that, while dismissing the notion of natural rights, he retained – unlike earlier critics – much of its content. Green found the doctrine of natural rights unacceptable for three reasons: it assumed that individuals brought into society rights that did not derive from society; it asserted that those rights could be held against society; and it detached rights from the duties individuals owed their society.[32]

Green could not conceive of rights except as emanating from social life, because individuals could attain their ends only through cooperation with others towards a common good. Rights could only be held by members of a society provided each member recognized in that common good a good for himself or herself as well. Hence a right was

> a power of which the exercise by the individual or by some body of men is recognised by a society, either as itself directly essential to a common good, or as conferred by an authority of which the maintenance is recognised as so essential.

If the term 'natural' were to be used at all, it would apply to fulfilling 'a moral capacity without which a man would not be a man' and to the necessary end that society had to realize.[33] For it was social life, and human development within its ambit, that were natural.

The social recognition Green alluded to was not that of convention or custom but one based on a mutual, rational appreciation of human agency and capacity for action, coupled with the realization that each person's free exercise of his powers depended on his allowing equal free exercise to every other member. Here was a central link between the idea of autonomy and rights. Green conceived of human nature as self-determining, self-conscious and as conscious of membership of a society. Thus any right had two aspects:

> on the one hand a claim of the individual, arising out of his rational nature, to the free exercise of some faculty; on the other, . . . a

concession of that claim by society, a power given by it to the individual of putting the claim into force.

These two-faceted rights were necessary to 'the fulfilment of man's vocation as a moral being, to an effectual self-devotion to the work of developing the perfect character in himself and others'. Morality was possible only on the basis of spontaneous and voluntary action and could not be imposed by external or legal fiat. Human nature contained the capacity 'for freely fulfilling some function in the social organism'. Force and law could only indirectly create the conditions for its attainment.[34]

Rights were thus moral claims for self-development but extended the concerns of liberal theory by their equal emphasis on the development of others. Crucially, Green argued that rights were concurrently powers 'claimed and recognised as contributory to a common good'; consequently, 'a right against society, in distinction from a right to be treated as a member of society, is a contradiction in terms'. Although this may appear as an aberration within the liberal tradition its rationale hinged upon a rational, benevolent and democratically agreed position on the common interest. Were such an interest capable of full expression no right could be alleged against it.[35] For Green a society and a state – ideally the harmonizer and regulator of all social relations – were potentially the ultimate guarantors of humanity, its natural sociability and its ability for mutual improvement; the rights within those communities enshrined those capacities.

Karl Marx

Finally, let us go back briefly in time to note Marx's highly influential critique of the very concept of rights. Marx attacked both the notion of human rights and of (legal) citizen rights, dealing with them most notably in the context of his examination of Jewish claims to political emancipation in Europe. Human rights were nothing but those of the bourgeois, 'the member of civil society, i.e. egoistic man, man separated from other men and the community'. Scrutinizing the French revolutionary declarations and constitutions, Marx reinterpreted the right to liberty as that of the separation of man from man, the right to property as that to the arbitrary disposal of private possessions, and the right to security as guaranteeing those commercial and capitalist arrangements.[36] The sale and purchase of labour power was the very stuff of the 'innate rights of man' where 'Freedom, Equality, Property, and Bentham' ruled together, based on selfishness, gain and private interest, yet ostensibly working for the common weal.[37] The egalitarianism of rights theory was rejected by Marx for failing to acknowledge inequalities among individuals, and reducing potentially all-round developed human beings to unidimensional workers.[38] In sum, human rights represented a false view of human nature, as selfish, and of the social structure, as consisting of isolated monads separated from the community.

As for establishing the rights of individual citizens, such political emancipation was for Marx a chimera. Because he saw human nature as that of a species being, existing through others, unspecialized in the range of its developing capacities, and expressing itself through action, the granting of political rights was an impoverished conception that merely emphasized the separateness of the political state and perpetuated human alienation. True, such rights formally acknowledged the collective framework within which people existed, for 'they could only be exercised in community with other men'. This was one of the embryonic qualities of future socialist society manifested by the state. None the less, this was not the 'completed and consistent' form of real human emancipation as species being. Ultimately, Marx saw citizenship as degraded to a means for the preservation of the egoistic rights of man.[39]

All this is not to argue that Marx was a crude objector to human rights or that he would have rejected all the substantive values they aim to encapsulate. Rather, he saw human nature as solely realizable through a transformation of human and material relationships. The protective aspect of rights, directed against other individuals or human agencies, which is so important to the liberal tradition, was unnecessary in his vision of society because the eradication of class conflict would remove what he saw as the only source of threat to human development and expression. Marx's unmasking of some of the ideological implications of rights was instructive, although he undoubtedly employed an excessively limited version of the concept to fit in with his critique of capitalism. Contemporary socialist views of rights still occasionally exhibit these tensions and reservations but they are reluctant to do away with the idea of rights altogether. Moreover, as will be shown in

Chapter 5, some theorists in the generation subsequent to Marx's death were prepared to travel on an alternative communitarian path and to suggest uses for rights that could help to salvage the concept from an exclusively individualist application.

3
The Natural-rights Paradigm: An Assessment

In order for a right to function optimally as a protective capsule it would ideally need to display a number of properties. In a perfect but unattainable world all rights would be clearly demarcated and surrounded by impregnable defences, theoretical and practical. First and foremost, inasmuch as we are dealing with a central political concept, they would need to be essentially uncontestable.[1] For example, there would have to be a single valid position on whether the protection afforded by a right is non-negotiable and unrenounceable by the rights-bearer. The contents of actual rights would then have to be spelled out precisely so that, for instance, the right to liberty would invoke for all the same types of permitted behaviour and the same restrictions, if any, on the exercise of liberty. Although many modern scholars will be sceptical, at the very least, about the possibility of eliminating definitional disagreements the theorists of the past who adopted the natural-rights doctrines in their many varieties accepted, indeed insisted on, such a possibility. For centuries rights-theorists tried to construct as invulnerable a case as possible for the existence and protection of fundamental human rights. They devised philosophical arguments and theories aimed at establishing beyond all doubt the nature of those rights. They then grounded that nature on unassailable or, at least, rationally unquestionable truths. The language of the eighteenth-century declarations, describing fundamental rights as 'self-evident', speaks for itself.[2] Those arguments were then linked to political arrangements whose objective was to guarantee their observance.

If an infallible and unfalsifiable case could indeed be made for the existence of clearly defined rights all political systems would have to be judged according to their ability and success in protecting them. The preservation of human rights could then plausibly take precedence over other conceivable political goals. A second additional property of rights consequently relates to their strength (or weight), i.e. their capacity to override a value that might conflict with their postulation. A right to free speech might clash with the goal of national security during a military emergency. How vital, it may be queried, is free speech when information could inadvertently be passed on to enemies? And how demoralizing and unconducive to maximizing the war effort would its suppression be? Put differently, a given level of cost, up to which a right is worth preserving, might have to be established. At the extreme, a right would be protected at any cost; but it is also possible to insist that it be preserved at a *high* but not at *any* cost, or for *specified* instances but not for *all*. Here are further dimensions for intense debate. The uncontestable, strong version of rights characterized the thrust of seventeenth- and eighteenth-century natural-rights theory. In modified form that theory wields considerable influence to this very day.

The natural-rights doctrine serves as a paradigm for a theory of rights, a test case through which to explore its advantages and disadvantages, precisely because the doctrine posits a comparatively pure and simple case for the existence of fundamental rights and a radical and very strong notion of what a right is. Were natural-rights theory acceptable it would resolve many of the problems relating to rights and terminate the need for further rational discussion on those issues. If, however, it failed to allay our doubts we should either have to search for alternative theories, discard the idea of rights altogether or accept some of its unavoidable weaknesses.

What is the consequence of attaching the qualifier 'natural' to the concept of rights? Does it strengthen the concept or weaken it? Natural rights, in their original form, may be traced back to natural law and natural law transports us back to the Greeks. The prologue to the story of rights thus begins with the search for regularities of behaviour that applied to all creations of nature, human beings included. It concerns answers to the question of how we know when human beings are acting according to their nature. For the Greeks, this required a norm that could determine how people ought to behave. Reason was generally assumed to be that norm. Significantly, a once influential book on the subject, Leo Strauss's *Natural Right and History*, is concerned with natural law far more than with natural rights, while engaging in a paean of praise for the Greek view of virtue and a sceptical assessment of neo-classical natural-rights theory. The concept of nature as applied to human beings antedates that of right.

Although historically the concepts of law and duty also preceded that of rights, this does not – as Finnis persuasively argues[3] – diminish the notion of rights itself. The Reformation and the Renaissance effected, in different ways, an anthropocentric trans-formation. Instead of seeking to establish the content of the natural laws that governed, or ought to govern, human beings, and thence their compliance with such laws, the question became how to ensure that the individual would be entitled to, and able to benefit from, their application. Individuals now claimed the right to enjoy the protection and succour of natural law.

This development may be explained historically as the *evolution* of the idea of rights to the point where they became fundamental aspects of human thinking and organization. Alternatively, they may be logically and implicitly inferred from earlier concepts of natural law and therefore it may be contended that rights were *discovered* once circumstances were ripe for that intellectual breakthrough. The third option, of *inventing* rights, cannot be entertained by the natural-rights tradition.

The philosophical implication of this development has been to replace the temporal sequence from positive law to right with a logical sequence from right to positive law. This is often referred to as a right-based theory, in which – as Dworkin has maintained – rights are the most fundamental *moral* category.[4] Raz has responded convincingly that right-based moralities are narrow because they exclude moral elements such as supererogation or virtue.[5] Moreover, rights-theories are ultimately based on an infrastructure of other concepts. Our definition in Chapter 1 saw a right not as the basis of an ethical system but as its enshrinement. As Sumner observes, 'a moral right cannot serve as the ultimate substantive ground for its own conventional recognition. For this ground we must appeal beyond rights.'[6] And Griffin notes, 'it is not the right to liberty that is basic but the valuable life, *on some conception or other*'.[7]

In its original form the natural-rights doctrine offered a powerful case for the existence of rights. First, it simply argued that human beings are born with them, that they are part of our initial equipment in the same way as our bodies are. Take away my nose and, although I will probably survive, I will be less than fully and perfectly human. Take away my rights and the same will apply (although the loss of my right to life may possibly result in my death). Specifically, a *common* core of human nature is defined by encircling it with a succinct list of natural rights. Those rights cannot be denied without a potentially critical loss of what constitutes being human. They are hence innate, inalienable and indefeasible, if not inviolable. Second, natural rights are pre-social. They are not the product of any social artifice, historical growth or political contrivance. Quite the reverse: political societies may be created for the very purpose of ensuring the recognition and enforcement of natural rights. Third, natural rights are absolute. They prevail over any other consideration that might deny their validity, applicability or range. They are non-negotiable; they cannot be whittled away, compromised or diminished. They must, in Dworkin's fertile phrase,[8] trump any other claim or value that conflicts with them. Fourth, such rights are universal. This follows logically from assigning them to people as their natural equipment. Hence all human beings, irrespective of time or space, hold them. No particular instances can deny their applicability. No regional, cultural, national or historical variations can be tolerated. In respect of being rights-carrying entities, as well as in respect of the specific rights they are held to carry, all human beings are equal. Any attempt to deny these arguments, or to tamper with the properties of universality and absoluteness, would be – it was assumed – potentially catastrophic for both individual and society.

The very force of this version of human rights is also its weakness. Indeed, the more inflexible a theory is, the less capable it is of adjusting to circumstances it did not or could not foresee or of recognizing internal inconsistencies and tensions that do not allow for easy solutions. For some theorists the properties of natural rights are chimerical because their stringency invites contradiction and the rigidity of their casing suppresses attempts to adapt them.

Innateness

The innateness of a human right raises severe philosophical problems. It is impossible to prove conclusively that human beings *have* rights in the existential or moral senses assumed by natural-rights doctrine. In other words, must the definition of a human being include the attribute of rights-bearing? And is respect for others a moral consequence of the idea of a person? Or is a right a contrivance added later to secure certain human attributes? Philosophers, in whose domain these questions fall, disagree on these issues. However, whether or not human beings have rights existentially or morally, it is very difficult to envisage long-standing social arrangements that dispense with the assumption that people 'have' non-negotiable rights.

Self-evidence

Three terms have commonly been used to describe innate natural rights: self-evident, inalienable and indefeasible. Their implications need further exploration. Recent attempts to revive the self-evidence argument have been provided by McCloskey and Finnis. McCloskey's analysis leads him to identify the human features which support the claim that human rights are self-evident. He contends that these self-evident rights 'can only be grasped by reflection on the nature of a person as a person' – namely as a rational, autonomous, emotional, imaginative and creative being – in order to identify a morally adequate response to that nature: the right to respect as a person endowed with those attributes.[9] Finnis explicitly accepts that self-evidence cannot be empirically demonstrated or verified but suggests that it should be viewed as an attribute of rationally acquired knowledge.[10] These principles may appear too vague to offer guidelines for political action. McCloskey's argument opens him up to the contention that the fruits of such reflection may, or may not, change considerably over time and geographical space. This unwittingly draws attention to the cultural and empirical roots of such rights and hence to the malleability of human attributes, the protection of which is then claimed to be 'self-evident'. We shall return to this theme when discussing universality. Finnis's notion of self-evidence may itself be faulted for its immunity to rational critique or for offering a suggestive theoretical method that none the less may not produce a single set of substantive rights.

Self-evidence could plausibly be decoded as grounded on dominant historical and social patterns of thinking about human nature and human purposes, patterns which masquerade under the guise of self-evidence. It would then be a highly conservative assumption that could easily be deployed to neutralize the possible questioning of a society's norms and rules. It is difficult to ascribe self-evidence to a right – such as the right to health – the contents of which may be partially contingent (e.g. upon medical knowledge). The proof seems to be provided, in such an example, by an appeal to empirical evidence.[11] Hence, even though the rights secured may be factually the same as those claimed through the self-evidence argument, rights may alternatively be described as protecting recognized fundamental human attributes or even crucial social interests that incorporate such attributes. This switch of emphasis may reflect a more useful, or attractive, or emotionally satisfying or historically successful manner (in terms of widespread support) of thinking about the way a community is organized.

The concomitant of invoking self-evidence is to project a world which evinces a very high degree of moral consensus and which asserts the complete unity of rational argument. In sociological terms, as well as in its intellectual paradigms, such a world will not display much diversity. The other way, as MacCormick has contended,

> is to offer rationality as a value absolute so far as it goes within a Weltanschauung . . . happy in the knowledge that if anyone presents *reasoned* argument against such a position, he is thereby estopped from denying the standing of rationality.[12]

This envisages a world in which diverse opinions are unavoidable, where they must pass justificatory tests but where such tests may uncover rationally defensible positions: a world of pluralistic ideologies.

Of course, to deny self-evidence is not necessarily to relegate rights to the realm of contingency. A hybrid which I call quasi-contingency may be a more appropriate characterization.[13] The counter-contention here is that it is possible to be more specific about fundamental human rights as long as the historical and cultural flexibility thus introduced is checked against acceptable qualitative standards of behaviour and scientific knowledge. For while the social recognition crucial to a right's *existence* will emanate from intellectual, moral and professional groups with acknowledged standing, the *content* of a right will reflect the reasoned values and the reliable information about human needs and functions those groups produce.

Some theorists contend that justified rights are norms 'independent of recognition'.[14] It depends on the version of recognition one subscribes to. If what is meant is a formal legal procedure, basic rights may certainly exist prior to or outside that framework. Gewirth, in a more moderate form, denies that a right depends *entirely* on recognition.[15] However, at the very least, recognition is a necessary – even if not sufficient – condition for a right to exist. We refer here not to legal recognition, nor to majoritarian support, but to considered acceptance by morally and intellectually conscious and knowledgeable people who pave the way for legal or majoritarian acknowledgement. It is sensible to assume that there cannot exist *at the present* a right that *no one* recognizes. Gewirth is correct in asserting that if someone denies the existence of a right this does not establish its non-existence. However, the following is also correct: for a right to exist now it is enough to demonstrate that someone other than the claimant, in a position to communicate his/her viewpoint, recognizes it. To further argue that this is a basic human right requires testing against prevalent moral and scientific understanding and gaining wider acceptance. The scientific persuasion will entertain assumptions about human beings that are empirically demonstrable, yet always open to contrary proof. Finally, recognition without a willingness to act so as to facilitate a right is insufficient. Reasoned recognition must be coupled with protection.[16]

If this is still too vague the reader will have to become reconciled to the impossibility of introducing for all instances determinate boundaries to social action or to the conceptual analysis that seeks both to understand and direct such action. This is not to dismiss the idea of boundaries; rather, it is to acknowledge their relative plasticity and the futility of constructing a theory of rights in which all boundaries will be rigid. To that extent the perfectionist and clarificatory drives of some philosophies are bound to be frustrated.

Inalienability

Inalienability lends itself to even more interesting decoding. Much of this pertains to the notion of choice and the idea of option rights, which will be investigated later. For the time being we can pose the recurring question of what kind of human being, and which social arrangements, are implied by a world in which rights are inalienable, i.e. cannot be voluntarily renounced and transferred.

The notion of inalienable rights was the product of a social and ideological system in which human attributes were people's property and property entailed entitlement and ownership. But property may also involve exchange, and natural rights were deemed too fundamental to allow for such exchange. The possession of a natural right had to be distinguished from exchangeable property.[17] Of course, it was also unacceptable for individuals to discard or to give away altruistically the human rights that were theirs. The first was an irrationally self-demeaning act; the second, supererogatory and possibly morally praiseworthy but none the less undermining the well-being of the giver. The language of exchange was, however, both central to and legitimate in nascent capitalist societies and rights-discourse had to be insulated from the predominant rules and behaviour of the existing world. This meant arguing that the exchange of rights for any other good would dehumanize the individual; consequently capitalist exchange relationships had to be forbidden when it came to protecting essential human attributes, on the grounds that such protection was not a marketable commodity. Thus rights were removed from the economic sphere, but only by forging an abstract conception of human nature that bore no relationship to the dynamics of everyday life. That abstraction could then be applied, similarly detached from the vicissitudes of reality, to a plethora of concrete situations. This characteristic, as we have seen, still damned the 'bourgeois' conception of rights in Marx's eyes, although it also shielded aspects of human essence from the process of commercialization.

Another way of expressing the above developments is to contend that 'rights rule out certain trade-offs',[18] i.e. they cannot be exchanged for something else. But what about special rights, which arise out of voluntary transactions between identifiable persons, typically in the form of contracts or promises, but are not indispensable to human well-being?[19] Those rights protect renounceable arrangements which demand that certain acts be reciprocated, i.e. rewarded by parallel complementary acts. These are not basic human rights but 'purchased' claim-rights of a peculiar nature: conditional, market-exchange and act-dependent rights. Above all, they are non-universalizable private arrangements. In sum, a right that can acceptably and legitimately be traded off is the converse of a natural right. It protects a quantifiable good that has no intrinsic value, that is the private possession of individuals without regard to a public good. The right is hence alienable.

The very need to assert the principle of inalienability,[20] however, while designed to safeguard the attribute of human rationality, indicates a belief in the limits of such rationality and evokes a particular conception of a human being. It points to an implicit mistrust of individual intentions and to the potential self-damage that individuals could render themselves. There can consequently be circumstances under which an individual may abandon essential attributes as well as renounce the rights which protect them. Hence it is a logical corollary that individuals may have rights against themselves – against the harm caused by such action – and that those rights may be enforced against them by a guardian state or society without the taint of paternalism. This has been argued with respect to the mentally ill, but could apply to other serious non-rational or irrational behaviour.[21] If individuals were always perfectly rational there would be no problem. But individuals may, in clearly circumscribed and rare situations, have to be secured against their imperfect rationality or flawed volition.

Indefeasibility

Indefeasibility is the converse of inalienability and refers to the impossibility of a person's rights being annulled by others. While inalienability is a restriction on the actions of a right-bearer, indefeasibility erects a hermetic barrier around a right and the burden of honouring it falls on the members of the society to which the individual belongs.[22] Implicit in the notion is a society in which individuals are liable to infringe the essential rights of others, and the consequent need to restrain them. This places a low premium on human sociability and gregariousness and in particular on the trustworthiness and motives of governments. There are two senses in which a right may be nullified. It may be voided arbitrarily. But it may also be lost in a manner considered legitimate by the society in question. It may be forfeited as a consequence of the actions or forbearance of the right-bearer. For example, a right of way over a particular field may be forfeited if it is not exercised at given intervals. This is a typical feature of contractual rights. Indefeasibility, however, signals that some (basic) rights cannot thus be forfeited; in other words, that they are unconditional. They are removed from the sphere of responsible and intentional action, action that calls for assessment as meritorious or otherwise, because they are seen as preconditions for such action.

But, we may ask, is there no justification for awarding rights on the basis of merit? The case for old age pensions was originally presented as a reward for services rendered to society by its members over their lifetimes. Although looser than a direct commercial exchange, it signalled that some basic rights could be earned and, by implication, could fail to be earned. Property rights, too, were frequently placed in the same category.[23] This proved to be an intermediate stage in basic welfare-rights theory, as important aspects of those rights were later made independent of qualifying behaviour or status and desert was replaced by need.[24] In contradistinction, the right to sustenance *above* a basic minimum may still be linked to tests of willingness to work and be designed as an incentive to elicit socially valued types of behaviour. The imprecision necessarily attached to assessing desert would invariably drag fundamental rights into the volatile haggling of the political market.

Whether rights are conditional upon resources is, of course, another matter that relates not to the existence of the right but to the practicalities of its realization. Some thinkers, like Cranston, argue that if the wherewithal for the fulfilment of a right is not forthcoming, it is untenable: 'If it is impossible for a thing to be done, it is absurd to claim it as a right.'[25] This is to confuse the existence of a right with its implementation in the first instance and with its maximization in the second. The implications of Cranston's assertion are again highly conservative, for the dice appear to be loaded in favour of existing arrangements and do not allow one to claim a right prior to, and independently of, its potential implementation. It is obviously impossible for a man to claim the right to fly like a bird. But in areas of liberty and welfare, the word 'impossible' frequently disguises an unwillingness to change one particular distribution of means in favour of another.

As for the comparative strength of inalienability and indefeasibility, this depends on the relative importance assigned to the inviolability of the individual versus the authority of social norms.

Some individualists, including some liberals, will tend to respect indefeasibility more, because they wish to grant individuals, rather than societies, rights over their essential attributes. Others, perhaps traditionalist conservatives, invest so much respect in the majesty of the law that they will see rights as defeasible because they are conditional upon such respect being accorded by rights-bearers. But they may not allow alienation of rights, such as the right to life. Tyrannies will deny both indefeasible and inalienable rights and it is only among reformist ideologies that an appreciation of the two will be found.

Pre-sociality

The assumption of the pre-sociality of natural rights has become a major stumbling block to the relevance of the natural-rights doctrine. What was philosophically and anthropologically fashionable in the seventeenth and eighteenth centuries ceased to be so from the nineteenth. As political and social theorists we can no longer envisage people independent of some social framework and hence find it unattractive to reason in terms of a move from a state of nature to a state of society. Arguably, this change of perspective does not damage rights-theory seriously. By the very nature of the emphasis of the social sciences on human interaction, political theorists are not interested in single individuals. They are interested in societies, communities, groups – however obvious it is that they are composed of individuals – and the relationships of individuals to each other and to these larger entities. A corollary of the definition of rights adopted above is that human interaction plays an indispensable part in the shaping of the concept and the practices derived from it. To talk about the right of a single person on a desert island is a solipsism that has no relevance to political theory. A right is plausibly the product of social interaction if we accept that all people are from birth members of some human groups. Some theorists would argue that such membership itself may be an alternative basis for entitlement. This is one, though not the only, reason why the term 'natural rights' is increasingly being replaced by 'human rights'.

Absoluteness

The question of absoluteness runs up against three types of complications. There may be a clash between two competing natural rights, so that the realization of one can only be attained at the expense of the other; there will be internal contradictions even in the conferral of any one natural right; and there may be occasions (examined in Chapter 6) when a natural right has to give way to another human or social value. Thus, for example, the indiscriminate pursuit of A's liberty to do what he wants may curtail B's ability to hold on to her property; for A may claim the liberty to take possession of it. It could be maintained that this merely infringes B's absolute right to property, rather than annihilating it; but the operational problems of absolute rights suggest that it is meaningless to assert them because there is no logical solution to the compatibility of two absolute rights which compete over arrangements for desirable human behaviour. The conflict of such rights will outlast conflict among persons; the former is essential, whereas the latter may be merely contingent.

As an instance of the second type, any individual's absolute right to the liberty to force others to obey him cannot coexist with anyone else's absolute right to the same, for there are bound to be people who are restricted by the unlimited licence given to the strongest member of that society. But another example illustrates the complications ensuing from contested interpretations of the right to life. If the right to life means the right not to be killed, any action other than self-restraint on the part of others is unnecessary. But if it also denotes an interdict on deliberately letting someone die, then the right to life may demand that others actively sustain it. It would entail a right to all necessary medical assistance, but as not all human lives can be maintained under conditions of unavoidable scarcity of medical treatment, choices will have to be made as to whose life it is preferable to maintain.

In other words, the more generous we are in our interpretation of the right to life, the more likely is its absoluteness to be overridden. As we spread the protection of human lives we paradoxically decrease the protective force. Even on a minimalistic notion of the right to life it cannot be maintained consistently in those cases of abortion where the mother's life is at risk, inasmuch as the foetus is considered to be a living creature. The right of life of the mother is then simply in a zero-sum relationship with that of her unborn child.[26] Much current rights-debate is concerned with situations that do not fall into obviously soluble categories. It is precisely the need to accommodate those problematic cases that requires the relaxing of a stringency capable only of coping with clear-cut uncomplicated issues. The absoluteness of a right can only apply when all claimable rights are compatible with all others.

A popular device for evading the inherent contradictions of absoluteness is to talk about prima-facie rights. While still acknowledging the prioritizing and protective aspects of a basic right this allows for exceptions to be made. Although a green wave of traffic lights entitles me to drive down a road exercising an orderly freedom of movement, siren-sounding ambulances are entitled to override my freedom by emerging from a side street even if the lights are in my favour. It may be thought that the prima-facie argument is a dangerous erosion of the notion of a valuable right and an opening to the possible annulment of rights by other considerations. This ought not to be so. As Vlastos contends, the burden of proof must always rest on the counter-claims to a prima-facie right.[27] To assert a prima-facie right is neither to deny its fundamental importance nor to signal that its upholding is not a duty expected of all. It is rather to suggest that a slightly weaker form of a basic right may in fact be a more efficient way of promoting what it protects. It recognizes that human relationships cannot usually be sorted out neatly; indeed, that to insist on the absoluteness of a right is to allow a single counter-instance to nullify it. For a concept to be viable it must be allowed to bend slightly when unbearable stress is exerted; otherwise it will snap.

Prima-facie rights still remain rights that should always be asserted, but the intensity of that assertion must take account of the possible damage that may be caused to other rights that protect crucial human attributes. As McCloskey correctly states, 'most commonly when a prima facie right is overridden, it is not overridden by good consequences, but by concern for other prima-facie rights.'[28] The clash between mutually damaging prima-facie rights will remain a problem which may only be sorted out by common sense or, indeed, fail to be sorted out satisfactorily. Obviously, these strictures pertain to rights in a zero-sum relationship; there may also be rights whose application to one individual will not diminish their application to another, such as the right to equal respect, discussed below. Such rights may therefore be designated absolute.[29] But the kind of world in which prima-facie human rights would be predominant is one in which all rights to all necessary things cannot be claimed; in which human beings are believed capable of exercising practical, not pure, reason; in which social relations will incorporate the flexibility required by a readiness to accept change, innovation and unpredictability; and in which sustainable compromise is itself a principle of community life.

Universality

Equality

The question of universal rights is not without its problems either. The first difficulty concerns its relation to the notion of equality. We need not enter into the complicated debate about the aptness of the notion of equality when comparing person to person. All we need consider is whether there is a case for according human beings equal rights. Two fundamental approaches are possible: we can identify crucial features that human beings share to the same extent, which therefore require the protection of rights; or we can argue that the differences among them are nevertheless the basis for equal rights. The first strategy is deployed by theorists who identify a minimum shared by all people, such as the need for nourishment or the ability to suffer pain. This substitutes the idea of a common minimum (although even that will vary from person to person) for the idea of equality in general, and locates human rights only in that common area.[30] The second strategy grounds such equality on the intrinsic dignity or worth of diverse human beings.[31] To accept that outlook is to argue for a conception of a person endowed with a moral core that exists independently of other, empirically determinable human attributes. It is then possible to argue that all human beings have a right to equal concern and respect, by allocating equal weight to each person's equal preferences,[32] or by acknowledging that each person has a separate life to live.[33] Both strategies may overlap through arguing that all human attributes, however varied, can only flourish when some fundamental conditions obtain. The rights of all to freedom and well-being are regarded as such conditions, and their equal bestowal is the rational consequence of this strategy.[34] So while identifying basic shared features, the rights that protect them also enable important human differences to persist.

The right to equal regard is a historically novel one and a good example of the conundrum concerning the discovery or evolution of rights. We tend nowadays to assume that people have always been equal in important respects and that the right to equal regard permanently safeguards important intellectual and emotional pre-requisites for human flourishing. This was not thought to be the case in the past and is thus an apposite instance of the quasi-contingency of the historical perspective on rights. A right will be *contingent* to those who see history as relativist, accidental and non-cumulative. It will, however, be *quasi-contingent* to those who regard history as evolutionary. For them, beliefs that only emerged at a specific point in time may become lasting even if their appearance depended upon a particular set of events that might not have come about. Both positions may be distinguished from the argument which regards equality as self-evident.

There are further categories that do not fit neatly into the description of fundamental rights as universal. The first category is that of specific human rights. I use the term 'specific' to distinguish these from 'special' rights, discussed earlier, which are neither basic nor unconditional. Specific human rights, on the other hand, are basic rights borne by particular classes of people, yet held against all. Pregnant women and new mothers may claim rights that men will never be able to claim. We may wish to designate them as formally universal: anyone entering such a class becomes a rights-bearer. Or we may relate them to an essential human need that requires protection and servicing. This latter option will, however, also include other rights-bearing classes, such as being elderly or ill, potentially open to any human being but not in fact held by all. Specific rights are not conditional on behaviour or merit. Broadly, the rights of child-bearing women may be predicated on their biological needs, or on the physiological and psychological re-quirements of small babies, or on the awareness that particular human groupings have differently valuable attributes, as with the cultural and national claims considered in the next section. This is what philosophers like to call an over-determined case: there is more than one sufficient reason for according rights to particular sets of women.

The second category concerns the right to special treatment consequent upon past discrimination. This is a distinctive right of a compensatory kind, based on past deprivation. Affirmative action may be claimed as a right in order to equalize human opportunities that were previously denied effective prioritized protection. Unlike other fundamental human rights this is a temporary right granted to individuals and groups which have been unfairly deprived of their ability to function adequately. Were such equal status to be achieved or restored, the right to special treatment would be nullified.

Cultural diversity

Theorists who prefer to suggest that there are, or ought to be, moral principles common to individuals will necessarily extend them to all communities because they regard the human race as the unit of analysis. These moral principles will then be the basis of rights.[35] But human beings are also guided by ideological beliefs and subject to differential cultural codes. If people were both identical and static in their wider range of needs, wants and attributes – physical, psychical, social and cultural – universality would be easy to defend. But if human beings are thought to hold only a bare minimum of characteristics in common then the more we seek to stretch their rights in time and space the thinner those rights become. The universality of a right cannot, on the most basic level, allow for the scarcity of resources, the range of natural attributes that pits rights-claimant against rights-claimant and the variegated cultural codes that help determine what people value.

Any discussion must hence consider the following possibilities;

1 If there are universal aspects of human nature essential to fundamental and wholesome human functioning, the rights that protect them must be universal.
2 If all societies share in common cultural and historical features essential to social function and structure and to the welfare of their members, the rights that protect these must be universal.
3 If there are either specific historical-relative features of individuals and societies necessary to their well-being, or divergences in their natures, the rights that protect them must be particular; although a second order principle may establish that there is a universal case for the institution and protection of such rights.

While there certainly are universal basic human attributes, such as the needs for food, clothing and shelter, other conditions for well-being may be culturally mediated, such as the requirement to worship a deity – a requirement that atheists will not evince.

Moreover, rights have in the past been predominantly claimed by individuals against their states, or their governments as agents of those states, while in the international arena states have claimed rights – mainly not to be interfered with – against other states. National communities, therefore, have used and developed rights-language in varying ways. Many theorists have argued that human rights are a Western ideological notion: that to choose the promotion of human rights rather than citizens' rights reflects – as Burke believed – thinking about an abstract universal community and imposes political structures, conceptions of the individual, and peculiar relationships between individual and community that are not generally shared.[36] These criticisms increase when concrete declarations of human rights are analysed, displaying salient biases towards certain kinds, and specific interpretations, of rights. It has been remarked that attempts to impose the 1948 Universal Declaration of Human Rights as it currently stands 'reflect a moral chauvinism and ethnocentric bias'.[37] Paul Ricoeur has observed that 'discussion of human rights, narrowly conceived as subjective, individual rights, becomes mere self-justification and subterfuge – an ideology, in short, as soon as it hides the violations of economic, social and cultural rights'. For him, 'the subject is now the people, as a cultural reality. Universality gives way to generality. Man is no longer whatever has a human face; the concept dissolves in the antithesis between the individual and the group.'[38] The revived appreciation of nationalism as a defining characteristic of large human groups has driven home the point that legitimate particularisms may serve important human ends and that their elimination may cause severe social dysfunctions.

But how then do we avoid sliding down the slippery path to a particularist extreme, where any individual or society may decide what its rights are? And does Ricoeur pose in reality a choice not between ideology and non-ideology, but between two competing ideological positions, the one attaching rights to traditional Western conceptions, the other interpreting them in the light of more recent knowledge, opinion and standards? The alternative option of postulating a common moral core is either perfectionist (if we wish to view it favourably) or static (if we do not). The choice seems to be between the imposition of standards of behaviour cutting across national boundaries, and between falling back on a stance incapable of constructing a case against the withdrawal of normal human rights from sections of a population, as in Nazi Germany. Hence the universalistic/relativist problem is how to obtain a strong enough notion of rights without freezing a particular ideological position, postulating an essentialist or ideal view of human nature, opting for a minimalist number of rights or dispensing with them altogether.

There is, however, another option. The notion of universality is better regarded as a moderate gravitational force that orders and attracts the concept of rights, rather than a powerful black hole that swallows up and annihilates them. An alternative formula would reflect both the fundamental character of rights as protecting key human attributes – interests, needs and capabilities – and the variety and possible evolution of such attributes. It would need to identify empirically determinable human attributes and acts that vary within certain ranges and form the bases of rights. The ability to suffer pain is one; a desire for liberty may be another. There may indeed be significant human attributes that are shared virtually universally; but it is equally plausible that time- and place-specific features are just as basic; and that they may reflect particular cultural and social developments either unique to a given society, or potentially replicable if circumstances are conducive. Such rights may slowly change over time and space as human attributes change; in fact many hardly do. To that extent their moral significance is related to universal attributes; but to the extent that essential human properties are culturally moulded, the latter will occasion a relativist morality and a changing rights-system. To suggest an *a priori* list of universal morals and allow diversity only with respect to the rest does not fundamentally alter the difficulties encountered by the natural-rights doctrine, with its fixed catalogues of rights.

Many rights are, of course, still being discovered or invented. The rights of women – both as human beings and women-specific – are still being spelled out in rights-compendia. Indeed, historically changing views of human nature have already applied to non-trivial attributes of women, or of homosexuals. Conceptions of women have evolved beyond the view that ascribed to them intellectual inferiority side by side with moral superiority. Homosexuals are currently engaged in the process of removing the label of moral perversity from their sexual proclivities. Yet in the past those descriptions seemed to many to be self-evident just as their obverse may now claim the status of self-evidence.

Importantly, rights may not only be added to a very flexible list, but may be shed; rights which were in the past perfectly valid, basic, ethically justifiable, radically liberating for the individual and socially beneficial may no longer be so. Thus in nineteenth-century Western Europe extensive rights to exclusive private property were widely perceived as a prerequisite to a tolerable life, although since then other institutional arrangements have limited their justification. The protection of rights relates to their perceived indispensability to human flourishing, independently of whether they are universal or not. Such universality is a byproduct of the fact that human beings share many important attributes and is not prior to empirical observations.

Modern rights-theorists would none the less like to couch rights – as did natural-rights-theorists, however faultily – in the most vigorous terms possible. How, then can they still construct a case for rights as strong protective capsules, if it may not be possible to fashion the perfect case for a right? To answer this question it would be well to proceed from the following proposition. The various properties of human rights (although not of all legal ones) – such as strength, the range of rights-bearers and irrevocability – cannot all be maximized simultaneously. The pursuit of one aspect of a right will in all probability only be conducted at the cost of weakening other properties it needs to display. The strength of a right, for example, may be obtained at the expense of the size of the rights-bearing population and vice versa. Decisions about this internal balance must involve the prevention of serious damage to the rights-bearer, as will be argued in Chapter 6, taking account of the particular circumstances of each case.

Choice and Welfare

Options and will

In this chapter we confront an inescapable fact. The peculiar nature of the concept of rights, as a capsule surrounding other social and political concepts such as liberty, welfare, interest and self-determination, makes it quite impossible to disentangle the analysis of rights from the properties of those client-concepts. Those properties will influence the way a right behaves and operates, and what it signifies in a social context, although it is also true that attaching a right to other concepts will profoundly change *their* interpretation. When we choose any one of the different meanings of liberty or welfare and assert it as a right, a vast range of other questions is posed: the desirability of state intervention, the realm of the private, who is part of a rights-bearing population, what degree of compatibility obtains among rights to different things, the question of paternalism – to name but a few. These necessarily elicit a variety of answers. To delve into all would result in a long volume not only about rights but about concepts that have been discussed in other books in this series. All we can do here is to give an inkling of some of the major issues.

As we have seen when surveying the development of rights-theory, rights emerged as defences erected round individuals, intended mainly to vouchsafe a space into which other individuals – including, most importantly, those representing the government – were not entitled to enter. This notion of forbearance may be deemed comprehensible and rational only when attached to particular views of human nature and social structure. To allow such unimpeded space is to suggest that the individual benefits from the non-intrusion of others. Hence it puts a high premium on the separateness of persons and a low one on the intentions of others as far as the individual is concerned and on their capacities to assist him or her. It also suggests that the individual is a good user of the space made available, which puts a high premium on the rationality of individuals with respect to their own ends. Finally, it suggests that such arrangements provide better benefits for society, thus putting a low premium on the direct and coordinated efforts of a society to pursue its own good.

Historically this perspective was a simple negative-rights one, implying (Hohfeldian) liberties with their concomitant of non-intervention by others. Hobbes, as we have seen, entertained no great moral or intellectual expectations as to what people would do with their liberty. Significantly, a change was introduced when the individual bearers of these liberty-rights began to be conceived as active in a specific sense – as beings capable of autonomy and choice. The idea of autonomy, adapted from Kantian philosophy, denoted the capacity of human beings to make rules for themselves; the idea of choice indicated a world of open-ended possibilities from which each person would select the alternative he or she preferred.[1] That choice was also assumed to be rational from the individual point of view. By now, the individual occupying the space cleared by negative rights was perceived to be the bearer of special endowments, namely, the capacity for agency and for an intelligent exercise of freedom. Negative rights were seen to protect those endowments.[2]

These latter features have become central for the adherents to the choice- or option-theory of rights, whose most salient modern exponent is Herbert Hart. In a famous article, Hart argued that if there was one natural right, it was the right of all people to be free.[3] Stated in reverse, Hart's theory runs something like this. The essence of being human is being moral. Morality can never be imposed but is brought about through choice and autonomy. Hence in order to be human and to express one's nature, every person has the right to be free. In a manner typical of some moral philosophers this theory was presented as a universal rule while its derivation from a specific conception of human nature was glossed over.

A more general argument is provided by Gewirth. In addition to the right to freedom, Gewirth establishes a right to well-being. Both types of right, however, have the same end: to ensure the conditions without which rational autonomy is impossible and without which human agency cannot be realized. Gewirth goes on to argue that because each individual, as a rational agent, is entitled to the liberty to pursue his or her good, all human beings are entitled to do the same for themselves.[4] Rawls, too, assumes in his hypothetical model, in which rights are somewhat peripheral, that they pertain to the primary goods – mainly civil liberties – that rational/moral individuals would regard as necessary to the functioning of a just constitutional framework.[5] Implicit in these arguments are three assumptions. The core of human nature is purposive action, self-control and self-development; agency and autonomy are the pinnacle of human existence and other human attributes and functions are secondary to them; all individuals are equal in their potential rationality and in the right to action emanating from it. The conjunction of the first two assumptions will make the task of welfare-theorists more difficult. While they have no rational grounds for denying that the identified components of human nature are indeed central, these may not be sufficient. They may wish to add other core human capacities, such as the capacity to enjoy friendship or music. The pursuit of human well-being need not then be demoted to instrumental status in relation to autonomy. The third assumption may be challenged on the grounds that the ends perceived by one individual as good may not be similarly perceived by others, and therefore the right to act cannot endorse the right to *any* action.[6]

Choice-rights, however, are handled in two very different ways, although the distinction between them is often blurred. So far we have discussed the centrality of the human capacity of choosing and the importance of giving it high priority and protection by conferring a basic-right status on it. But another approach to choice gives individuals the option to exercise, or not to exercise, any right they may have. I may have a right to adequate heating in the winter, but choose not to claim the payments which I can use to keep myself warm. The difference is a significant although simple one: between a right to exercising the specific capacity to choose, and a choice over whether or not to exercise any right.

This latter right is related to the Hohfeldian subdivision of a right into a power, and has once again received its clearest treatment from Hart. For Hart, a right bearing a correlative duty is a power that right-bearer A exercises on right-upholder B. The potential upholder is under the sway of the right-bearer; a decision of the latter will determine the former's options for action. On this understanding, a right may be waived. A permanent waiver will involve forgoing the right and transferring its control to others and is effectively indistinguishable from alienation. But a temporary waiver may merely signify that the right-bearer refrains from claiming a right in a specific case. Hence, the notion of 'waiving' confers ultimate sovereignty on the choice-exercising individual, irrespective of the consequences of such waiving, and develops an idea of rights emanating from private agreements or quasi-contracts.[7] This is hardly surprising in view of the derivation of the right-as-power conception from Bentham's theories.[8] It also weakens Hohfeld's distinction between powers and liberties, as even liberty-rights assume that individuals exercise powers.[9]

The notion of A's control over B introduces power relationships in a way that, under extreme conditions, may be manipulative. The discretionary aspect[10] of such rights establishes an optional dimension of upholding (albeit determined by the rights-bearer) that could undermine the fundamental nature of many rights. This is a highly individualistic and personalized view, entitling individuals to decide on the protection of many of their fundamental interests and capacities; in other words, it decentralizes and privatizes the pursuit of some beneficial human ends. Moreover, and at least as significantly, Hart describes such a right as a species of normative property,[11] thus drawing the concept decisively into the circle of capitalist ownership, with its presumption of exchange value as well as its asymmetric preference of the self over others, of alienability over defeasibility. *Laissez-faire* social relationships are the logical concomitant of these principles.

Now, of course, a different question may arise here. I may have the right to waive a right, to choose not to exercise it; but do I have the right not to exercise choice in general, that is, not to be rational and autonomous? And is it necessary and desirable to give me such control over the rights I may want to waive? Here the choice of the rights-bearer is balanced against an interest that may not coincide with that choice. In order to maintain that people can waive rights without suffering dehumanization we must assume that human beings behave rationally with respect to their basic rights or that they will choose to further their non-egoistical interests. Another weighty question is not only whether individuals should have the right to waive rights (this conflicts with the related arguments for inalienability) but, correspondingly, when rights-upholders should be morally bound by such waiving. We can only expect them to bow invariably to the will of rights-bearers if we postulate a society in which mutual concern and responsibility are not behavioural norms and in which rational action cannot extend beyond oneself. Some socialist theorists would therefore prefer to deny individuals the power to waive rights.[12] Alternatively, we may release others from the duty to be bound by an individual's wishes in such matters.

Here it may be useful to distinguish between:

1 A right that it is not wrong for someone to realize; and
2 A right that is necessary for human flourishing.

This bifurcation appears at first close to Golding's differentiation between option-rights – concerning freedom and choice – and welfare-rights – concerning entitlement to some good necessary to well-being.[13] There is however, one important distinction. Although a particular option-right may be waived, it is still necessary to human flourishing that human beings have the rights to freedom and choice and be able to exercise them over an acceptable range. The reasonable, if not absolute, control over one's life that rights afford is a core constituent of individual well-being.[14] Although liberty-rights may seem optional, their existence belongs to Golding's welfare-rights category.

Right (1) is similar to Hohfeldian liberties, whereas right (2) pertains to fundamental human rights, and the general exercise of choice must on any account be such a right. Right (1) will logically include right (2) (because it is not wrong for me to flourish) but will also include less central, or weaker, rights. It will include behaviour that is optional in the sense that its non-performance will not damage the person. Right (2) may be secured possibly even against the wishes of the rights-bearer because it is deemed to protect necessary human attributes; right (1) entails protection against possible violation by *others* only, against defeasibility but not waiver or alienability. That kind of protection would be necessary but not sufficient to guarantee right (2).

There is an an interesting historical backdrop to this debate. For Hobbes all rights, including that to self-preservation, include the option of forbearance. Yet at the same time self-preservation does not appear to be optional. This tension, argues Tuck, was only removed by an alternative radical tradition that insisted on non-renounceable rights, which led to the later notion of inalienable rights.[15] The addition of the idea of inalienability (embryonically in the radical tradition of the seventeenth century, emphatically in the eighteenth) is of great historical significance precisely because it diluted the choice/forbearance notion of rights and attached them instead to essential and rational human wants.

Hart is more aware of such problems than some of his critics acknowledge and has therefore excepted some fundamental freedoms and benefits, relating to the security, development and dignity of the individual, from those rights whose operation, even existence, is determined by individual choice. He has done so by applying to them the Hohfeldian category of immunities, although with respect to adverse change only.[16] Another way of approaching this is to distinguish choice-rights from Benthamite benefit-rights, which confer advantages that accrue from other people's obligations.[17] The purpose of this distinction is to highlight the notion of a right as something due rather than something claimed or exercised. However, this involves two unfortunate implications. First, that to exercise one's choice is not to one's benefit; second, that the object of such a discharged obligation will always benefit from it. The latter objection disputes the inevitability of the two steps according to which the beneficiary of a duty will desire its discharge, and that such desire will necessarily be in his or her interest.[18] Thus, while the concept of 'benefit' is more confusing than helpful, because all rights are intended to be beneficial,[19] we are still left with the concepts of 'choice' and 'interest'. Neither has a clear edge over the other, nor is the exclusive adoption of either costless in terms of promoting certain human values.

We conclude that it is possible, and may be necessary, to have both kinds of rights. Two assertions follows:

1 A particular instance of an optional right may be waived, but not the right to optional behaviour as such.
2 The range of option-rights may be restricted, because the permanent waiving of a right to protect necessary features will be dehumanizing – hence inalienability must be insisted upon.

There is one further distinction that has to be considered: that between waiving a right and discarding the object/value the right protects. For example, the waiving of the *right* to life may not be an acceptable option – in the sense of my no longer being able to control my choice to live inasmuch as I can control it. But I may choose to kill myself (possibly violating my right but not abrogating it). Similarly, I may choose to be unfree without waiving my right to liberty. If I wish to regain my freedom, my right to do so is unimpaired and must override any rights other people may have obtained over me as a consequence of my giving up my freedom. If, however, I am understood to have a duty to uphold my basic rights, I cannot be allowed to violate them. That entails social arrangements in which external social norms occasionally predominate over individual choice.

How does this apply to suicide and euthanasia? Do these practices waive a non-optional human right? Permitting them appears contrary to the assertion that the upholding of human rights may be forced on individuals, that their rights must occasionally be protected against themselves – in order both to ensure their flourishing and to serve a vital social good – and that the choice to forgo them ought not to be available. Feinberg distinguishes sharply between alienating and waiving. For him, waiving the right to life, as distinct from alienating it, does not incur its permanent renunciation. However, the issue is not simply that of who controls the ending of life, but what to do when the maintenance of one human right (life) becomes intolerably costly in terms of maintaining other human rights of the same person (e.g. freedom from suffering). Waiving the right to life is in this instance a decision to end the infringement of other human rights beyond the point where the rights-bearer is dehumanized. Feinberg discusses that only in relation to the right not to be born of a foetus whose future interests (e.g. health or adequate care) cannot be preserved.[20]

Interests and needs

The area of welfare-rights, too, displays a diversity of approaches that can illuminate a range of ideological positions. In general, welfare is associated with the satisfaction of needs, of desires or of interests.[21] But a right to what individuals need is not the same as to what they desire or want. I may need additive-free food I do not want and I may want a limousine I do not need. We may conclude that I should have a right to have my needs satisfied yet hesitate whether that right should be enforced when I do not desire and claim it. Alternatively, my recognized right to purchase a limousine will obviously decrease in importance in comparison with rights to things I need and it may be heavily hedged with restrictions to ensure that more important needs, for others as well as for myself, do not get trampled on in my eagerness to acquire a big car. Yet it may also be contended that I *need* to have some of my *wants* satisfied, even if they are not strictly necessary to my functioning. The fulfilment of desires is a psychological and emotional need which will have to be accommodated to other needs I and others have.

'Interest' is thus a more useful term than 'needs' or 'wants', because it can contain both, while not resolving the tensions between them. If something is in one's interest it will be advantageous. If it is also fundamentally so, it requires rights-protection.[22] However, two problems arise. First, the term 'interest' is itself frequently used to indicate selfish desires, as shorthand for self-interest. That connotation may lead to the underplaying of interest as a non-selfish attribute; and for reasons of clarity alone, there could be a case for jettisoning the notion of interest-based rights in favour of a broad interpretation of welfare-rights (just as the concept of natural rights has been discarded because of similar connotation problems). Second, if something is 'objectively' in one's interest it could be imposed paternalistically against one's will. Hence rights-bearers' interests must include exercising their ability to make informed, rational choices.[23] A viable rights-theory must exist somewhere between the two ideological extremes: the Scylla of conservative paternalism and the Charybdis of libertarian acclaim for all choices.

A common version of welfare relates it to *material* assistance to individuals *in need*, but is also concerned with a *fair* redistribution of the resources available in a society. The two are not identical and one may fall short of the other. The material aspect of welfare associates it restrictively with the distribution of quantifiable, aggregative goods, frequently in the form of public assistance programmes.[24] But it is one thing to argue that a fair share of available resources is a human right and another that securing the broad needs of people is. The first case suits a variety of liberal-reformist and socialist positions by contending that people have a fundamental claim on the bounties of nature and society, because without enjoying them fully, or at least having full access to them, human potential will not be achieved. However, existing societies also create and market goods whose human benefit is debatable, and a fair, let alone equal, distribution of such resources may be quite pernicious. Do we really want full and free access to guns, for instance? The second case falls foul of the 'limitless needs' issue, which conjures up the spectre of an insatiable and all-consuming individual. The fundamental prerequisites of human functioning are borne in mind but problems of scarcity mean that we may have to opt for very basic needs or acknowledge that needs may always outstrip resources. A secondary problem will be the possible forgoing of universality, unless our distribution system is a global one. Those who maintain that this is unavoidable may also concede that most welfare-rights are civic, not human,[25] although, as we have seen in the previous chapter, the notion of human rights is tenable across geographical divides.

Both the satisfaction of needs and the fair distribution of resources involve providing people with property, in the form of consumption of goods, or their use and possession. It is generally agreed that the right to property is fundamental in that sense, namely that people require exclusive ownership at least over some basics, such as food, and use-rights over other goods without which their personality cannot be expressed or their flourishing guaranteed.[26] Only libertarian negative-rights-theorists, however, regard a wide range of exclusive private-property rights, grounded on consent, as both basis and manifestation of individual liberty;[27] other ideological positions are more concerned with the provision of important goods than with the question of their formal ownership.

The broader view of welfare-rights proceeds from the notion of 'claims to the goods of life'[28] and extends welfare to cover all needs and capacities that are essential for human functioning. This requires breaking down into two questions: not only our perennial one about the implicit view of human nature, but one about the meaning of welfare. When human nature is epitomized by the notion of rational agency even advocates of welfare-rights tend to interpret them as ensuring the provision of needs basic to such agency. Of course, the list may be a generous one: physical necessities, health, and education will figure predominantly.[29] Rational choice and purposive action are impossible, on this argument, without creating the conditions for their realization.

Inevitably, though, a hierarchical conception is now brought into play. The preference of moral philosophers such as Gewirth for extolling the human capacities for choice and autonomy over other human attributes means that the physical, emotional, psychological and mental capacities of people are seen as mere servicers of the moral essence of the individual. On this understanding welfare-rights are complementary to choice-rights but operate on a subservient level.

This stringent prioritizing of human abilities and characteristics is decodable in ideological as well as philosophical terms. Such a reductionist view of human nature will accord preference only to a basic equalization of opportunities, in which provision will be made for whatever is deemed sufficient for people to exercise their choice and autonomy. It will rule out any external assistance in the making of the choices themselves or in the working out of individual 'life-plans'. And it will relegate many types of human activity to a lower status, as means to an end. Even if those means are considered necessary, they may conceivably be substituted on occasion by other means.

The alternative extension of welfare to encompass every aspect of human well-being would *include* the choice and self-determination that give vent to our moral capacities. Although the common distinction between choice-rights and welfare-rights is often intended to demonstrate the superiority of the former as the more adequate conception, that assumption would be challenged. There would now be no need to supplement welfare-rights with (rational) choice-rights. Rather than channelling welfare-rights into autonomy-rights, the former would swallow most of the latter up. What would be left are option-rights of the contract or promise type – effectively, special rights – that are not basic to human flourishing.[30] This is evidently the case if two steps are taken: welfare is attached to the concept of interest, and that concept is purged of its conventional association with private interests-cum-wants alone. Implicit in that approach is a human being with broad and equally valuable capacities, who would suffer serious deprivation if those capacities remained unnurtured, and whose good is furthered by a generous view of welfare-rights as promoting all aspects of his or her well-being, subject only to a reasoned recognition of what that well-being currently constitutes.

The use of such terminology exposes some of the difficulties relating to the differentiation of welfare-rights and choice-rights.[31] First, it underplays the network of concepts and ideas in which rights are located. The preference for one type of rights-conception over another may crucially depend on the conceptions of human nature and social structure brought to bear on the issue. Second, it is by no means inevitable that the two types are in a purely competitive relationship, so that the promotion of welfare could only be effected by restricting liberty or withholding the right-bearer's control.[32] Rather, it is plausible that autonomy, too, is in one's interest and a constituent of one's well-being. Third, the converse does not hold, either. The internal structure of rights-concepts is such that on any construal they will contain some components that are in a competitive relationship, so that no conception of welfare-rights is capable of maximizing all its elements. Total autonomy is as chimerical as total welfare; hence less than perfect autonomy must be regarded as a social and political inevitability – from some ideological perspectives, even as desirable. There would then be no *a priori* reason for assuming that the pursuit of imperfect autonomy would lead to a greater good than the promotion of other aspects of human welfare.

Fourth, the distinction between choice and autonomy must be amplified. It does not follow that any and all restrictions of liberty-as-choice necessarily curtail autonomy, as some types of choice – e.g. a decision to sell oneself into slavery, or the consumption of a mind-numbing drug – may be harmful to autonomy as well as to welfare. The exercise of choice *per se* cannot be seen as adequate compensation for the loss of other human values such as self-determination and health. Indeed, the socialist critique of *laissez-faire* is based not only on its inegalitarianism but on the liberty-constraining effects it has on the worse off.

But is not the 'right to be wrong' one of the legitimate aspects of choice? Strictly speaking, it is not a right at all, as it could hardly be argued that being wrong is a valuable, rather than a simply normal and probable, human characteristic. More plausibly, it is a liberty-right to make mistakes rather than a right to be wrong *simpliciter*. Such a right does not *centrally* protect the capacity to make rational choices, as mistakes – although they are a useful way of learning – are not the best way of being rational. It is rather an acceptable, perhaps inevitable, cost of exercising choice and may protect individuals from other unacceptable costs – damages or retribution – of exercising that essential capacity.

Because welfare-rights are claims for action that extend beyond forbearance and are intended to supply the rights-bearer with resources, they are interventionist and therefore sometimes described as 'positive' rights. They require others to pass judgements on individuals' needs and capacities and deliberately to do things that influence the ways such individuals will act. Initially positive rights seem difficult to accommodate to liberal values because of the paternalism they may be thought to invoke.[33] Some theorists support the primacy of non-interference because they define human beings chiefly as project pursuers.[34] Liberalism has, however, come to adopt quite easily, and indeed logically, the more generous notion of human nature discussed above. For even granted that non-intervention protects one's moral capacities, intervention may be far more important in protecting one's physical and emotional capacities. Those who collapse human rights into moral rights blur the distinction between protecting the specific moral capacities of people – their right to be moral – and protecting all human capacities, which is, in a general sense, to act morally towards people by respecting their rights to function and flourish. Even scholars well disposed to welfare-rights assert that 'to be a liberal is indeed to believe *inter alia* that nobody should ever be forced to pursue his own good'.[35] But, as we shall see in the next chapter, liberalism has aligned itself with communitarian social theories that transcend its former strict individualism and permit controlled intervention.

The notion of welfare interests endorsed here does not simply entail superimposing such interests against an individual's will. Although that might happen under carefully prescribed circumstances, normally individuals will, on reflection and information, be able to associate directly with, and want, interests they may not originally have been aware of. The forced imposition of an interest must, as usual, be hedged with qualifications relating to the harm and benefit to the individual and to others as a consequence of that enforcement. Beyond that there is the issue of the interests of groups of which the individual is part. In addition, as Plant has noted, even negative forbearance-rights involve commitment of resources, e.g. taxation, the marshalling of which requires state intervention.[36]

There is yet another way of approaching the welfare-rights issue. Which conception of social structure entails a non-interventionist notion of rights and which an interventionist one? So far we have been operating within a framework of a broadly individualistic network of human relationships, in which people enter into mutual voluntary agreements, while a large area of private space is retained round each person. As one non-interventionist rights-theorist, Fried, has put it in Benthamite terms, 'society has no special right to choose [values], since society, after all, is only the hypostasis of individual, choosing persons.'[37] This atomistic conception of society emphasizes the personal integrity (for which, read separateness or independence) of the individual, whereas the activities of the social body surrounding that individual are perceived as potentially threatening to him or her. In parallel, the assertive and initiative-taking aspects of human nature are opposed to the dependence and vulnerability of people. Indeed, if a right is seen only as a protective device for a self-sufficient individual, and not also as an enabling injunction to assist a mutually dependent and cooperative individual, it will reflect an ideology of conflict in which people are potentially hostile to each other. Thus, although the atomism of social structure is analytically independent of the possible selfishness of human nature, the two are in effect conflated. The result is an inherent ambiguity in rights-theory which suggests simultaneously that human beings are worthy entities deserving of respect and that they are mutually endangering entities for which rights could be a last ditch defence.

Fried would therefore debar the violation of negative rights understood as 'the right not to be wronged intentionally in some specified way.'[38] This raises interesting questions. First, because not all harm to individuals is intentional who, if anyone, is responsible for unintentional harm? If, for example, John is injured in an earthquake, or develops totally unforeseen side-effects twenty years after a course of treatment with a particular drug, intentional harm can evidently be ruled out. But the dehumanization precipitated in the first case by a natural cause and, in the second, by a series of human actions, results respectively in a condition identical to that which would have been caused by deliberately blowing up a building in which John was residing or using him as an unwitting guinea-pig for medical experimentation.

From Fried's viewpoint no right has been violated because the desirable model of human interaction is one in which conscious, aware individuals enter voluntarily into mutual transactions. Only such individuals can commit wrongs, and in the examples given above no wrong has been committed. Second, Fried elevates the satisfaction of wants, linked to the capacity for choice and the formulation of individual life-plans, above a general satisfaction of the needs of all members of a society, suggesting further that money is the correct measure of such wants.[39] It is of course vital to recognize the right of different people to develop along their various paths and to choose their personal projects.[40] But not *all* paths deserve encouragement. The burden Fried's scheme puts on people's rationality is immense. Not only does it assume that individual life-plans will be beneficial by definition but it also assumes that the price people place on their wants will be equivalent to their value *for* them, not merely *to* them. I may assign high value *to* owning a compact disc system and be prepared to fork out a considerable sum to purchase it. But the worth I assign it is not necessarily identical to the value it has *for* me (it may damage my ear-drums, I may fail to develop my musical appreciation through it or its purchase may reduce the money available to me for other goods).

John's rights reflect this free-enterprise, market notion of human conduct and are meant to perpetuate the conditions that enable it. But from the extended perspective of welfare-rights, John has the right to whatever is necessary to his wholesome functioning. Two things follow from this. First, if it is considered intolerable that John must suffer helplessly as a result of the unintentional acts of others, or defects of social organization, or non-human factors beyond individual control, we may insist on rectifying such dehumanizing circumstances. That means that a right has to be upheld in one of two ways. We can maintain that irrespective of the cause of an injury, an unconditional duty falls on specified others to prevent such harm to John; or, because that is generally asking for too much, we can insist that compensation be given to John so that his dehumanization will be balanced or minimized as far as is feasible. This latter possibility is based on a distinction that Fried does not consider. Interests may be adversely affected through impersonal and unintentional factors and events that do not themselves constitute an infringement of human rights, but that result in a situation in which individuals may claim goods as a right emanating from their subsequent deprived condition. In Chapter 5 we shall examine who the rights-upholder is in these cases.

Second, the evaluation John puts on his wants may be overridden not only because they may be harmful to others – a position nega-tive-rights-theorists on the whole accept – but because they may be harmful to him. Whether or not the conclusion is to deny him a right to such wants is, as we have seen, a complex issue. Civilized so-cieties deny individuals the right to consume some debilitating drugs at will but they currently merely signal strong disapproval of the consumption of nicotine. They may devise economic arrange-ments to make the rights to some goods costly to implement thus creating an ideological pecking order among forbearance-rights. All such wants are regarded as equally valuable by the negative-rights-theorists who claim that 'instead of propounding one imper-sonal standard of value invariant among persons, impartiality at this level recognizes as many standards of value as there are persons, each one providing reasons for action to that person.'[41]

Positive rights, on the other hand, have a dual intent. They demand action on the part of others, and they demand such action specifically in order to secure an acceptable standard of well-being. On the whole positive rights are ideologically attached to a maxi-mizing perspective, requiring whatever intervention is considered necessary (while seeking, as a matter of high priority, to secure the rational assent of the individual to such intervention) and aspiring to maintain a position anywhere between adequate human func-tioning and human flourishing.

The reason why action on the part of others is demanded relates to a communitarian view of social structure, in which mutual depen-dence is the norm and in which human personality, needs and conduct are shaped through social interaction. The very idea of intervention may then be a misnomer, for it becomes a necessary rule rather than a untoward exception. On this understanding in-dividuals cannot function without the cooperation of others, and therefore membership of a society is itself a fundamental human need that demands protection. Deprived of such membership and its benefits human beings cannot exist, let alone thrive. On this understanding, also, the regulation by a society of its members is a necessity of social organization, as is permanently institutionalized mutual assistance. To ensure the well-being of individuals, 'inter-vention' in their lives may be necessary. Moreover, because of mutual social ties, this may have to be secured through 'intervention' in the life of others as well. Without those actions, the satisfaction of human needs, the opportunities for their self-expression and the coordination of human conduct are considered to be impossible, although to a sceptical observer this may merely appear to be unjustified interference in the private domain. This view will be considered in greater detail in Chapter 5.

Rights-bearers and rights-upholders

The issues addressed by the debate on choice- and welfare-rights have led, among others, to diverse emphases on the attributes that human beings are thought to possess. The pluralism surrounding the question of which core attributes need the protection of rights poses two further crucial questions: which groups or populations bear rights and against whom? A shift in the cluster of attributes will not only change our understanding of what it is to be human but may include or exclude entities who share some, but not all, of whatever properties we designate as core human attributes.

A number of theorists assume that only human beings can be rights-bearers.[42] This is a concomitant of identifying the capacity for autonomy and choice as (1) uniquely human and (2) of such overriding importance in what constitutes a human being as to assign it higher priority for rights-status than any other characteristics human beings display. This position, as we have seen, regards human beings primarily as moral entities who therefore require the freedom without which morality cannot be exercised.[43] Such a restriction is an unnecessary and complicating one, in particular because it causes insoluble boundary problems. Are children, especially babies, rights-bearers if the capacity for choice and autonomy is the basis of a right? Are foetuses? Are mentally handicapped adults? And are other forms of life, such as the more intelligent animals, or all living things?

The problem is twofold: which human attributes need protection by means of a right, and what is our position if some of those features are shared by non-humans as well? To attempt to respond to the first issue we need not, of course, deny the centrality of the capacity for autonomy and choice as defining human characteristics. All we need do, as we have seen, is to query what the grounds are for ranking that capacity as superior to other human attributes or, more accurately, as more necessary to human functioning. The alternative is to regard human beings as clusters of diverse properties and potentials, physical, psychological, emotional, mental, *as well as* moral, each of which is necessary to being human. To rank them is impossible without introducing further considerations that do not emanate from the nature of a human attribute. To suggest that some are more worthy of protection by a right is to deviate from the definition of a right provided in Chapter 1. Consequently, the pursuit of human welfare cannot distinguish qualitatively or policy-wise between protecting people from freezing; safeguarding them from harassment and threats for the purposes of extorting information; providing them with,[44] or at least not denying them, opportunities for expressing and receiving love; obtaining the educational tools to make rational, or at least informed, decisions; and securing areas free from external intervention when they make choices that do not damage themselves or others.

The protecting or enabling of any one of these interests is a sufficient justification for according rights to human beings. This is a point of great significance, because it offers a multiple rights-strategy. Obviously, if we regard people as packages of diverse properties, they will only flourish when all the human rights attached to those packages are guaranteed. Notwithstanding, any human being that can be shown to have at least *one* of those properties is a rights-bearer, for each and every property is essential to his or her functioning. Consider the rights of very young babies. Clearly, they are incapable of rationally informed choices or of acting as autonomous beings. Hence they fail the agency/autonomy test of rights-bearing ability, because they are not moral entities in any meaningful sense. Some moral philosophers try to escape this difficulty by regarding young babies as *potentially* moral entities. But this is a weak argument. If potential for moral and rational conduct were the ground for a right, it would certainly exclude other categories of human beings such as severely retarded people, who do not even have this potential. Hence the agency/autonomy approach can actually diminish the range of rights on offer. If however we amend our strategy and define a rights-bearing population as one capable of pain and suffering, then the right to protection from these dehumanizing and debilitating conditions or, if humanly possible, to their alleviation occupies centre-stage. The result of this is to change the scope of that population. There would then be no problem about including babies, as well as mentally retarded people, but we might have to include *all* sentient creatures. This is not to assume that moral properties are not equally demanding of protection by rights for those who display them – namely, all normal adults. Rather, this offers a pluralistic approach to rights that maximizes the protection and enabling of important human attributes.[45] An individual would need to pass only a single test of eligibility out of those on offer in order to qualify as a rights-bearer.

What is the position with regard to foetuses? Feinberg is right to remark that the question of whether a foetus has a right is not primarily normative but conceptual.[46] It, too, revolves round the issues of moral capacity, physical needs and more generally of interests. The distinction between the rights-bearing status of babies and foetuses is relevant only to the early period of foetal develop- ment[47] when life is unsustainable independently outside the mother's body (although new medical breakthroughs have pushed that boundary back). This is why abortion presents such a complicated challenge to the rights-analyst. Those who deny that the (newly formed) foetus is alive will not grant it rights. But those who believe that the foetus is a living entity may still not unequivocally claim rights for it. They may simply run into difficulties when attempting to identify the specific interests a foetus may have; even more than with babies, almost all such interests can be depicted as potential; alternatively, their denial will not unequivocally cause it suffering and certainly will not stunt the expression of human capacities. But assume now that the fundamental right of life claimed on behalf of the foetus is threatening the right of its mother to life. In this case the life of one entity is, unusually, in an unavoidable zero-sum relationship with that of another. By assigning rights to the foetus we render a solution to the problem impossible; any decision taken is a logically arbitrary one, and pragmatic considerations external to rights- theory will have to sway it. Paradoxically, then, the ostensibly humanitarian extension of rights to foetuses may diminish the rights of other rights-bearers: their mothers.

We can now stretch the argument further. From all the above, there is no inherent reason why rights should be based on *exclusively* human characteristics, nor is there an analytical need to separate human beings strictly from other potential categories of rights-bearers. While political and social theorists will understandably concentrate heavily on human beings and therefore on the rights *they* may have, there is no reason for them to deny the existence of an overlap between humans and non-humans. The capacity for pain and suffering is one that human beings share, for example, with rabbits. This does not make it therefore less of a human attribute, merely not an exclusive one. Furthermore, because the actual capacities of young babies and rabbits are less demarcated than those of young babies and adults, if we accord rights to babies we may claim rights on behalf of rabbits, too. This argument differs from an opposing tendency among rights-theorists to contend that human beings owe duties to animals, but that animals do not have rights. Not surprisingly, that tendency typifies choice-right-theorists, who can of course point to the fact that animals cannot exercise autonomy, nor constitute moral communities together with human beings.[48] They may regard the cost of predicating rights on the physical capacity to feel pain and suffering as unacceptably high because this would not distinguish between humans and animals, and would dispose of a right as a valid claim that entails a conscious awareness; in short, it would undermine the implicit value-hierarchy that locates human beings alone at its summit as bearers of special and superior qualities and impair the promotion of a right as a unique enshrinement of human worth.

In the light of the more inclusive approach to rights adopted here, the consequence of denying them to animals is intriguing. It suggests that the features and capacities animals have are not deserving of protection as a right and that to the extent that they are shared by human beings the latter cannot claim them as rights either. We thus reduce the range of features and capacities whose protection human beings may claim as a right.

Finally, an observation on the revised conception of human nature that emerges from this discussion. To talk about human rather than natural rights is to link rights with human nature in a non-traditional manner. It does not imply that human rights spring forth fully clothed from an objective, or even sharply defined, notion of human nature. Human nature itself is, in all of its aspects, the product of human interpretation as much as of biological, chemical and environmental processes, although some attributes are more durable over time than others. In this very significant sense the human nature on which rights are grounded will itself

always remain a construct of the human mind, and rights will never be merely reducible to the bundles of human aptitudes and needs that constitute us as living entities. And although it is not necessary, as we have seen, for rights to *protect* the capacity of choice alone, it is nevertheless true that in a second order sense both the *existence* and the *content* of rights will always be a matter of human choice.

Human Nature, Development and Community

The historical emergence of rights is inextricably linked to the rise of individualism. But as the notion of the individual itself underwent important modifications, the rights attached to the individual experienced parallel change. The individual as unit of analysis was retained but acquired greater sophistication on three different dimensions: as a complex, multi-faceted bundle of capacities, as subject to a pattern of evolving and maturation, and as interwoven in significant ways with groups and communities.

In the previous chapter the first dimension of this three-dimensional basis of human rights was explored: the multi-faceted view of human nature. It was suggested that all human attributes, not merely those exclusive to human beings, require consideration, that it is arbitrary to prefer one facet to another and that a full appreciation of the range of human needs and capacities supports an extended rights-theory. This chapter will examine two further dimensions in which human nature and social structure may be analysed. The one relates to a developmental interpretation of human nature; the other to various theories of communitarianism. What follows will be an alternative view to the one dominant in current rights-literature. The purpose, however, remains that of teasing out the ideological assumptions at the bases of rights-discourse. While that process will certainly be directed towards unmasking hierarchical, static, non-communitarian conceptions of human nature, it will equally apply to the argument I proffer. It is therefore no more 'correct' or 'true' than any other. All that can be said is that it is a plausible alternative, one that can be asserted with no less scholarly rigour than its competitors, and one that ultimately – as with all social theories – must be judged by its intellectual and cultural attractiveness. Indeed, the very availability of more than one basis for rights-theories is itself a pluralist good that liberal societies salute.[1]

Development

Whereas seventeenth-century rights-theorists employed static models of human nature, the eighteenth century, with its theories of progress, and the nineteenth century, in which compelling evolutionary perspectives were grafted on to those theories, saw the rise of a conception of the individual that was strongly developmental, occasionally teleological and sometimes even determinist. At the root of these views was a belief, well known to the Greeks but now reharnessed to the cultural tastes, social theories and scientific evidence of the day, that the unfolding of a range of attributes was central to the natural processes of growth with which human beings were endowed. On the more determinist part of that continuum the individual may not have had a major part to play in these processes, so that the question of rights was not a salient one. But when the question of progress and evolution was thought of as open ended, a reflection of individual lifestyles as well as species needs, it was agreed that the stifling of such growth and maturation, or even their artificial rechannelling, could inflict considerable harm on individuals as well as impairing the prospects of their societies.[2] In particular, the concept of liberty was reformulated to include a continual ability to express and exercise the developmental nature of persons, and any impediment to such development, whether caused by deliberate or unintentional human actions, or by non-human factors, was construed as a constraint on the free working-out of natural capacities. Because liberty was a well established right in its older sense of non-intervention in the actions of a person, these new ideas helped to extend the concept of rights in an important direction.

The break with individualism was most effectively accomplished in a once popular book by the Scottish philosopher D. G. Ritchie, *Natural Rights*. Ritchie's critique of natural rights is still remembered because of his ethical and utilitarian reassessment of the type of human nature enshrined in that doctrine, but he contributed originally and decisively to all the above-mentioned dimensions. On the issue of development Ritchie's strong interest in evolutionary theory provided him with what he considered as empirical evidence for earlier theories of progress. He wrote that 'it is only with the progress of time that we discover the natural gifts of an individual or of a society.' The development of those gifts had to be included in the end of the state – by which he also implied a rational community.[3]

The right to the development of one's nature is of course open to more than one interpretation. Some theorists will introduce an intervening factor, namely that such growth, not only physical but even mental, moral and emotional, is also natural and inevitable, in the sense of being independent of human volition. Others will more positively see that development as self-determined, as a function of the exercise of the individual's own will, or what used to be called character. Both groups will therefore subscribe to the right to liberty from any intervention in that process, intervention which would merely undermine the conditions for such wholesome and desirable growth. They will then converge upon the autonomy/ agency view of rights, and regard such liberty from intervention as a precondition for exercising the human capacities it facilitates. Hence that negative-liberty-right will have priority over any other right human beings claim.

Undoubtedly human intervention may negatively affect the rate of growth of key human faculties. But this is not logically entailed. It is equally conceivable that intervention may assist that growth. Indeed, if the purpose of human rights is, among others, to ensure the fundamental process of human development, and if such development can only be effected through the enabling actions of others, there is a case for the right to whatever assistance and cooperation is required for individuals to mature and grow. Nor does this imply unrestrained, or paternalistic, intervention. Rather, the rights to liberty and to welfare will be deployed in parallel, as and when fit, in order to secure the realization and flourishing of human potential.

The much used notion of flourishing itself reflects the emergence of numerous sophisticated theories of human development – cultural, social, intellectual and psychological – over the past two hundred years, and their increasing complexity. Feinberg, for example, sees within human nature 'latent tendencies, direction of growth, and natural fulfillments'. He relates flourishing to flowering, growing and spreading, to the progression of interests to their harmonious fulfilment.[4] Griffin has posed the choice between rights as necessary for human status and necessary for human flourishing – human life and good human life.[5] The first would assume a static conception of human nature and could require rights to minimal political participation and freedom of conscience; the second, a developmental or evolutionary one, catering specifically for dynamic human attributes, such as the right to education or to nourishing sustenance.

This flexible view of rights reflects the elasticity of the attributes they encapsulate. A major advantage lies in its introduction of a historical dynamic that protects it from quick obsolescence, as our understanding of what it means to be human changes. For human beings may not only develop new capacities, they may shed old ones, or they may retain capacities that we no longer want to enshrine as rights, such as the capacity to enslave prisoners. A major disadvantage mirrors the fear that the good life is too extensive, the rights it invokes too broad and the contents of those rights unlimited. On the individualist side of the ideological spectrum it is then objected that rights to 'all-consuming needs' will 'interfere excessively' with the rights of others to pursue their life-plans, because they will be called upon to redistribute too many of the goods they presently own.[6] Once again, needs will be challenged in the name of wants. On the collectivist side of the spectrum the opposite will apply, as rights to maximum wants, even if they are not directly pernicious to the well-being of others, will be challenged in the name of needs.[7]

The indeterminacy of rights apparently resulting from an extended version of necessary goods leads some theorists to complain that the concept of a right loses its discriminatory force altogether, as virtually all goods that contribute to human flourishing may then be claimed as a right.[8] This is more of a practical than a theoretical objection. There is nothing in the logic of the concept of rights that will restrain it from covering an unknown quantity and unpredictable range of benefits that human beings will at some point think essential to their flourishing. Even the right to adequate functioning, rather than flourishing, leaves us no wiser, as the notion of adequacy is capable of being similarly stretched. Ideas concerning the minimum level for dignified living have undergone massive changes over the past 150 years. All we will be able to say is that adequate ranges and scopes of rights will be less than those required for full flourishing.

Nevertheless, there is a practical danger that some rights may impose unbearable demands on a society's resources and thus devalue the concept. We are already witnessing the competition over resources occasioned by the right to health and the problems connected with the distribution of that right. Expensive heart surgery limits the amount of capital and labour available for more conventional medicine. Feasibility and fashion rather than principle limit the implementation of such rights. But this has no bearing on whether our decisions are qualitatively correct or based on ranking those health-goods that deserve rights-protection. The complications attendant on distinguishing between so-called basic health and luxury health are part of the incommensurability *vis-à-vis* trade offs question we shall examine in Chapter 6.

These problems cannot be dispensed with. But they can be mitigated by treating rights not as logically indeterminate notions but by operationalizing them on the basis of an adjustable culture- and science-related appeal to those aspects of human nature that are known to need special cultivation and protection. If in theory an issue has no resolution one has to choose between abandoning it and offering a substitute solution. As in this case philosophical analysis offers no solutions, and inasmuch as a solution is necessary for purposes of the efficient, even minimal, functioning of a society, we have to seek guidelines from cultural and social behaviour recognized as rational and as moral. If the growth model is reasonable on those lines it could provide a dynamic conception of rights that is in principle sustainable, with societies distributing their resources fairly among those rights perceived to claim practical urgency. But practical urgency is not to be confused with a final judgement on the priorities of rights.[9]

Community

In recent years there has been growing acknowledgement of the role of groups in rights-theory and, correspondingly, of what are termed 'collective rights'. It is now a commonplace to recognize that societies consist of identifiable groups that may bear rights, or may be required to uphold them. That category includes families, ethnic groups and trade unions. As Gostin has observed, 'the dynamics of collective organization take on a significance of their own. The conception that groups should have only those rights possessed by their constituent members is a fiction.'[10] The ideological backdrop to that approach is one in which pluralism is a social norm, in which free association is a vital means of human expression, and in which political power and social interests are forged by balancing the static entrenchment of group interests with a dynamic group competition over national ends. But this approach to groups curiously omits, with singular consistency, the group that contains them all – society. A prominent reason for that omission is that state and society are not always clearly distinguished. The traditional hostility that rights-theorists display towards the state, as a power apparatus threatening its individual members, is unwarrantedly extended to society, of which the state is only the political manifestation. Moreover, the rights of smaller groups have been most commonly debated in the sphere of civil rights, as collective rights asserted 'against unreasonable government interference',[11] although the rights of minorities may equally be directed against social and cultural practices in general. Conversely, the notion of the global community is beginning to gain ground, especially with reference to basic subsistence-rights that individuals claim against humankind, though the real addressees of those claims still remain governments or voluntary agencies.

A further sense in which collective rights have been construed does indeed relate to the greater social whole, yet continues to do so in individualist fashion, and is found in the burgeoning field of public-goods literature. A public good is one that when distributed will be available to, and benefit, any member of the public. An example would be unpolluted air. The public, however, is conceived simply as a collection of individuals, all of whom are included in the provision of the good, and strictly speaking such goods cannot be claimed as 'inherently collective rights'.[12] This approach cannot effectively cope with discrimination against individuals which treats them as undifferentiated group members rather than as persons – for example, American blacks. The attribute, however trivial, they are made to share is designed to single them out as a group and override their individual characteristics. It is thus common to talk about groups in a sense very different from collective users of goods.

This takes us some way, but not far enough, along the path towards the concept of community, with its evocation of society not as an aggregate of individuals but as an interactive entity that reflects and enhances human sociability. We have seen in Chapter 3 that societies intrude continuously on rights-debate, either through a questioning of universalism, or as the objects against which individual rights may be claimed, or simply as the medium or context through which individuals associate and apply their rights. But the concept of community may exist at a deeper level than implied by the basic assertion that human beings are social animals. In fact it may exist on two such levels. The first, weaker, version would contend that mutual sympathy and interdependence direct people towards cooperation, so that individual development and expression are impossible without sustenance, support and moulding by others. The second, stronger, version would contend that human beings are entities whose essence lies in their group membership. The analytical emphasis then shifts to the nature of the group and the features and attributes *it* evinces and their bearing on the constitution and actions of group members.[13]

Before we examine the differences between these versions, let us consider their similarities. To begin with, such theories might conceivably accord rights a diminished role. If interdependence is a normal facet of social organization and mutual concern is a fact of human psychology and disposition, the potential danger of individual to individual that libertarian negative-rights-theorists warn against may be the exception rather than the rule. Consequently, rights cannot be justified primarily as protecting the free actions of individuals from the interventions of others because, as we have seen, such intervention may be beneficial and desirable, occasionally necessary, to the functioning of those individuals. One must, of course, be wary of swinging too far in the other direction. Those who place too high a premium on human sociability may end by denying the very purpose of individual rights, emphasizing instead the unlimited benevolence, rationality and concern that human groups and societies will display towards their members. Utopian and anarchist as well as totalitarian thinking can take that direction, thus removing the debate from the parameters of liberal humanism.

Following from the above, communitarians will bring into play a concept of social structure that regards individuals as essentially interacting rather than atomistically discrete, so that forbearance-rights become neither absolute nor even prima-facie rights. This is not to argue that regard for individual ends is not central to liberal communitarians, but to suggest that both forbearance *and* intervention may be used by them to promote such ends. Communitarians will attach rights to the furtherance of those aspects of human nature they value most, aspects which will certainly benefit from access to all the rewards of social life. As the liberal theorist L. T. Hobhouse put it, 'freedom is only one side of social life. Mutual aid is no less important than mutual forbearance, the theory of collective action no less fundamental than the theory of personal freedom.'[14] Moreover, much communitarian thought is attached to the notion of welfare-rights rather than choice-rights. Although there is no exclusive connection between welfare-rights and communitarianism,[15] there are two explanations of possible links. First, it is a sociological commonplace that the bounties of nature and society – to which a full notion of welfare will lay claim in the name of all human beings – can only be produced and distributed by social cooperation. Second, if welfare is an end that includes liberty but extends beyond it, many of its aspects can only be catered for through intervention in the lives of individuals.

This intervention will take one of two forms. The first may involve entering individuals' space by supplying them with goods or benefits. Sometimes, as in the case of compulsory vaccination during an epidemic, or the outlawing of the private sale of the organs of one's body, those benefits will be insisted on irrespective of the views of the individual concerned. As Feinberg has noted, this provides a way out of the question whether rights with respect to oneself also impose duties on oneself. He suggests that individual rights which impose duties on the bearer may more convincingly be justified as the rights of *others* to the upholding by rights-bearers of their own rights.[16] As those others are not specified, this can become a communitarian argument.

The second form of intervention involves interference in the actions of the 'others', the suppliers of welfare, on whom individual welfare is dependent. The stress on fundamental rights as benefits as well as opportunities is a result of an understanding of human nature as vitally dependent for its expression on the actions of others, on what Raphael calls recipience from others.[17] This will sound rather different if the frequently pejorative terms 'intervention' or 'interference' are replaced by 'mutual cooperation' or 'interdependence'. Such mutuality should certainly not dispense with all negative rights, for space round individuals will still be necessary for important aspects of exercising their faculties. Nevertheless, many mental, emotional and physical attributes also depend on a social environment, and require the kind of protection that negative rights cannot offer. Much communitarian theory assimilates the developmental perspectives and the fuller range of human attributes examined above. Consequently, restrictions are placed only upon actions that detract from the human ability to develop and flourish in conjunction with others. That apart, intervention in others need not be an intrusion; it can contribute to their capacity to function physically, mentally, emotionally and morally.

On this view societies accept the responsibility for doing all they feasibly can to maintain and enhance their members' well-being. Three reasons can be enumerated for that. First, if they were not to do so their members would ultimately be dehumanized, being incapable of full development on their own and needing, as they do, cooperation with others in order to draw out their social capacities. Individuals may therefore claim the right to such social activity as a condition for their own humanity. The costs that such rights incur for others reflect an ethos of mutual responsibility. Furthermore, because people are particularly dependent on communities, the latter have strong obligations towards them – an argument analogous to the parent–child relationship without its attendant paternalism. Second, many constraints operating on individual action and development are the product of social malorganization, error or incompetence. Individuals may claim the right not to suffer for avoidable occurrences over which they as individuals had no control, and society may have a duty to compensate them for such occurrences.[18] Third, and here we arrive at the strong notion of community mentioned above, the protection of individual rights serves specifically *social* interests, such as national viability or the health and quality of working power available to a society. There is even a social case for compensating individuals for ills beyond social as well as individual control, such as droughts or earthquakes, as society is a prime beneficiary from the abilities and contributions of its members and their diminution will impoverish it. These strong support-demands from others are located nearer the socialist side of the ideological spectrum. From this perspective a right constitutes a claim that directly or indirectly enhances the quality of life *in* a community and *of* a community.

In one weak notion of community, also held by T. H. Green, individuals alone are rights-bearers. Social membership and citizenship are regarded as a necessary condition of that status.[19] In another weak version, those characteristics of human beings that display socially supportive conduct, creativity and cooperation are thought to deserve special protection by means of rights. Many scholars sympathetic to such communitarianism argue, not without reason, that 'a community consists of and is nothing apart from its members.'[20] At the same time, community membership engages human attributes that cannot be realized outside the context of a community, that depend crucially on cooperative action. To that extent, individuals are inseparable from their communities. Yet the interests of the community are not identical to the interests of its members *in toto*, but only to two types of interests: first, the interests of its members that depend on cooperative communal action or that are moulded by concerted behaviour; second, those individual interests the pursuit of which will benefit the community at large.[21] Hence it makes sense to talk about communal interests and rights that may need to be defended from those aspects of individual thought and action that are separatist or egoistical. Because people's interests, resulting from their existential status as members of a community – that is, over a circumscribed range of their conduct – converge and are identical, it is possible to refer to these, in shorthand, as the interests of the community.

Recent American communitarianism, such as Sandel's, is close to the above line of argument. But while trying to escape from the notion of the individual primarily as a choice-maker, it still retains a version of the self whose *self*-understanding is shared by other selves. For Sandel, this is the strong notion of community.[22] But there are stronger versions yet.

In what is here called the strong notion of community, society itself is seen as an actor and – crucially for our purposes – as a bearer of rights. It is important to distinguish this assertion from theories about the rights of representatives or agents of societies, such as the doctrine of the divine right of kings or the more familiar argument that states and governments have rights against members of their societies. In view of the historical emergence of individual rights as a shield against the arbitrary actions of rulers, the view that rights

may be held by entities other than individuals causes understand-
able anxiety. Humphrey, for example, contends that because states
are the greatest collectivities, to accord them rights that have
priority over those of individuals is to load the dice even more
heavily against the latter.[23] This is a narrowly legal or institutional
view. True, states and governments, wielding immense power,
frequently abuse the rights of their members and their restraint and
control is justified. But societies, not states, are the fundamental
collectivities and those on which human beings depend primarily for
their own functioning; and it is the case for *their* right to protect their
attributes that will now be considered. States are specialized social
organizations, whose needs and interests cannot be identical to
those of society, although societies that sustain democratic states
aspire to ensure a reasonable match and to render their states
accountable.

Indeed, as Tuck has observed, for seventeenth-century thinkers
such as Suarez an entire people could already count as an
individual, be an agent and dispose of its liberty. The later Levellers
also accepted that societies might be the subjects of rights.[24] But
these communitarian theories, also evident in Grotius, are seen by
Tuck to place rights in a subsidiary position,[25] and he subscribes to
an approach that, ultimately, situates state or community rights in a
zero-sum relationship with those of the individual. Many nineteenth-century thinkers, however, saw things differently. Ritchie
continued Green's remarkable transformation of rights-language
towards a radical extension of the naturalness of rights. He argued
that:

> if there are certain mutual claims which cannot be ignored without
> detriment to the well-being and, in the last resort, to the very being of
> a community, these claims may in an intelligible sense be called
> fundamental or natural rights. They represent the minimum of
> security and advantage which a community must guarantee to its
> members at the risk of going to pieces, if it does not with some degree
> of efficiency maintain them.

The assertion of specific communitarian claims, relating to the
nature of human society and ensuring its adequate functioning,
indeed survival, is the message to be read in conjunction with the
protection of individual rights. This perspective of philosophical
Idealism – the individual in and of society – heralded the dual theme

of human-rights-discourse that significantly helped to underpin twentieth-century welfare-thought.[26]

While Ritchie is frequently acknowledged by modern rights-analysts as a trenchant critic of natural rights, he is often ignored as the formulator of an important synthesis between rights-theory and utilitarianism. The latter survived as a dominant aspect of modern welfare thought because it shed its highly individualistic Benthamite aspects, as well as its quantitative calculus and 'the assumption of the identity of human nature in spite of differences of time and place and stage of growth'.[27] J. S. Mill had modified classical utilitarianism importantly, but Ritchie's contribution was more central. He saw morality as 'the conscious and deliberate adoption of those feelings and acts and habits which are advantageous to the welfare of the community' aided by the process of natural selection. Hence, 'in Ethics the theory of natural selection has vindicated all that has proved most permanently valuable in Utilitarianism'. Rights were one such element, valuable according to the empirical and historical test of utility – the general welfare – judged as it was from the social viewpoint.[28] The result was a new doctrinal hybrid – social utility.

Other liberal theorists took up that theme, contending that societies had distinct ends, interests and capacities to which rights pertained. The traditional individualist right to property, for example, was one that societies could also hold, for 'the claim of society to property [was] based on the ground that society is a worker and a consumer', as J. A. Hobson argued.[29] His colleague Hobhouse emphasized this from a different perspective: 'if private property is of value . . . to the fulfilment of personality, common property is equally of value for the expression and development of social life.'[30] Thus a clear 'view of the rights and needs of a society' emerged, required for supporting 'the full healthy progressive life of the community'.[31] Non-Marxist socialists similarly endorsed societies as bearers of property rights. The rights of a community must also be distinguished from what are commonly called 'social rights' which really apply to individuals, such as the right to leisure or financial assistance.

Even this strong notion of community does not invoke a detachment of the community from its members. It suggests that the nature of group dynamics will create needs, interests and actions that cannot be reduced to those of any single individual. But to avoid any misunderstanding, the possibility of a community claiming rights *in lieu of* its members must be ruled out emphatically. Human rights will always be vested in parallel in individuals and in their community and will exist on a dual level. This liberal communitarianism is far from regarding individual rights as less secure or important than communal rights. It will, of course, aspire to a possible and desirable harmony between community and individual needs, interests and actions. If such harmony is not forthcoming, rights-conflicts between individuals and their community will have to be resolved by the same constitutional processes used in adjudication between individuals. Clearly also, the agencies (including the state) set up by communities to tend to their interests will have to be subject to extensive democratic control.

In one area of debate modern rights-discourse is quite familiar with the rights of communities: the rights of states in international relations and law, as well as more recently the rights of peoples.[32] The most familiar theme here concerns the right to national self-determination; but references to it are ambiguous. On the one hand, the rights-bearer is clearly not an individual, occasionally not even a state, but a community assumed to act with a common purpose. As Raz points out, self-determination is one of a series of public goods to which societies have collective rights.[33] Communitarian theorists such as Taylor see self-determination, as well as the preservation of a language and a culture, as rights that can be claimed on behalf of communities.[34] On the other hand, it is a particular kind of community, one that appears as such only in the international arena, and the specific right to self-determination is itself clearly circumscribed. The international arena is still mainly perceived as one of individual actors (nation states), and self-determination is the exercise of each unit's right to independence in relation to external rule or influence. It therefore comes as no surprise to see libertarian politicians strongly advocating national rights *vis-à-vis* other societies and adopting the plural form 'we' when reifying the perceived interests of their society.

The point of this discussion is that there is no intrinsic reason to assign rights to individuals alone because there is no iron-clad case for arguing that only individuals are actors – and hence analytical units – in the socio-political sphere. As long as we subscribe to the ideological assumption that individual and community are normally mutually threatening and hostile, or at least that the overbearing influence communities exercise over individuals is paternalistic and stultifying, the centrality of individual rights must be paramount. But if we allow for a community whose thriving is dependent on the health and welfare of its members, yet one that may still offer ideas and policies for wholesome development beyond individual vistas, our view of rights will be modified. There will decidedly, none the less, be ample need for individual rights when those are violated by other individuals, and against groups and community agents who will violate or overlook individual interests. Importantly, any notion of community must come to be adopted consciously by the individuals who constitute it. It is then likely that the areas where individuals will still have to *insist* on personal rights will shrink, but such rights will never have to be alienated to the community.

Under such circumstances, if communities (or indeed other groups) have rights, there is nothing to prevent them claiming those rights not only against other communities, but against their own members. Inasmuch as communities require goods and services without which they cannot survive, such as labour power or the capital and skills necessary for ensuring the physical and environmental health of the next generation, they may claim those as rights against members who may not adopt the same social perspective. The outcome of this argument is to legitimate action on behalf of the community, in the name of *its* rights, to extract what is its due. We can thus conceive of two types of such legitimate social intervention in individual lives. The first would apply when crucial social interests are at stake. The second, discussed earlier,[35] would apply when crucial individual interests are at stake but the individuals concerned do not or cannot take the required steps to safeguard those interests. The prevention of individual dehumanizing is then both a direct humanist gesture and, indirectly, one of social utility grounded on the communal interest.

Rights and duties reconsidered

The relationship between rights and duties underlies many of the issues in this book. It would be a neat way of presenting that relationship if it were possible to demonstrate that every right has a duty and every duty a right; in other words, that the two concepts were correlative, as with Hohfeld's claim-right. It would also support a world-view in which human relationships were clearly delineated, mutual responsibilities plainly outlined, and reciprocal expectations known. Such a prospect is far too schematic and orderly, indeed dogmatic; it also elevates the sphere of rights and duties to that of a defining and controlling feature of human association. Rights-analysts have convincingly argued that not every duty entails a right, as the very notion of duty contains supererogatory elements, such as those associated with private charity, that are not met by corresponding rights.[36] But is it possible to argue conversely from rights to duties, so that a right will always entail a corresponding duty? The answer will depend on the types of duty we believe are necessary to uphold a right, as well as on our conceptions of human interaction.

Few theorists insist on tight correlativity across the board between a right and a duty. One reason for that is the common worry that rights could be expressed entirely in terms of duties, thus removing the point of a separate rights-language.[37] As has already been pointed out, this concern is unnecessary. More central to the correlativity thesis is that it appears to apply to peculiar kinds of cases. It is no accident that most examples of correlativity imply, as Lyons observes, specificity and determinacy,[38] and that, as McCloskey notes, they pertain to voluntary acts in which 'a person enters into a promise, contract', whereas 'more evidently, basic moral human rights and duties are not correlative.'[39] In other words, correlativity indicates a right we have already met before, a special right that is a product of human choice, that is endowed with the traditional contractarian features of rights, and that is consequently a private transaction among individuals. Many legal rights are prime examples of such transaction-dependent rights, with their strictly attached duties. Those contracts and the rights that safeguard them are normally conditional, so that the right and the corresponding duty may lapse if certain conduct is not forthcoming on the part of the rights-bearer.

These characteristics appear to rule out strict correlativity between rights and duties as an attribute of a *human* right. But this is only so if we adhere to the stringent requirements that some philosophers stipulate for such a relationship. Those who deny that rights necessarily have corresponding duties usually refer to the absence of a specific response to a Hohfeldian liberty right.[40] However, although liberty-rights do not demand duties to *enable* their exercise, they demand duties of another kind, namely abstention from intervention in the exercise of a liberty.[41] On the surface, this seems to endorse a negative-rights view of duties. But many contemporary negative-rights-theorists, following Hohfeld, do not even identify that correlate as a duty but define it instead as a no-right.[42] In so doing they refuse to endorse the possibility that liberties exist in social networks. They maintain that a liberty is an entirely atomistic right to act, or desist from acting, without reference to anyone else.

It is possible to insist that all rights, liberty-rights as well as claim-rights, have related duties when adopting a different ideological vantage point that introduces a far more sociable view of human relations. What disturbs those who query the usefulness of the strict correlativity thesis from rights to duties is the possibility that, if applied on a wide scale, it will generalize the obligations that correspond to any right. This generality may relate both to the nature of the attached duties and to the rights-upholders (or duty-bearers). Take my liberty-right to wear jeans. What duties do others have with respect to that right? Clearly, the basic duty not to interfere with my right to wear them. But what about the duty to supply me with them or at least to make them available for me? The issue of the appropriate right-upholders applies not only to liberty-rights but to claim-rights that are fundamental human rights. If my starving neighbour has a right to subsistence, does he have it against me in particular? And if not, are we talking about rights *in rem*, against the world? Is there such a thing as a right that no one in particular has a duty to honour?

We must therefore assess whether a right with such diffuse duties is feasible, and if so, what social arrangements it would involve. Such a right is feasible if

1 Rights can entail indeterminate duties.
2 Non-interference is regarded as a duty and a legitimate method of protecting liberty rights in general.
3 We can substitute another entity for the particular individual who may deny he is the upholder of someone else's fundamental right.

Condition (1), with its idea of indeterminate duties, is inimical to legal and some philosophical viewpoints but not to social and ideological analysis. Baier, for example, has usefully suggested that changing obligations are the key to understanding the contents of rights-theory over time. Instead of predicating the conceptual extension of rights he proposes to regard a right such as that to health as constant, but its correlative obligations as modifiable with changing requirements.[43] An altered version of that argument would suggest that as our understanding of what is encapsulated in the right to health changes, both the claims and the obligations required to meet it will undergo adjustments. So the sequence would then be *from* spelling out what we value, *to* a right, *to* the duties necessary to realize it. The two notions, that of a rights-package, and of its transformation over time, could thus be accommodated.[44]

Condition (2) is met when those who are unduly concerned about the *logical* relationship between rights and duties interpret a right as something that imposes specific types of conduct on others in defence of human attributes or capabilities.[45] This *social* consequence of a right has already been built in to our definition of the concept. Both action and inaction, when stipulated in relation to another's condition or conduct, require a deliberate response, an act of will. A liberty-right to appropriate money on a deserted road entails the duty of others not to prevent the first individual who wishes to from so doing or penalize him for it; in other words, to secure his right so to act without prohibitive and dehumanizing cost. Otherwise we would hardly need to talk about a right.[46] (It may be queried whether individuals do not have a prior moral duty to attempt within reason to ascertain the previous owner of the money, who may still have a residual right to it.) As Narveson has put it, 'There are not two separate problems, one of discerning the rights, the other of establishing the obligations. This one problem, of course, is a tough one. But at least there is but one.'[47] This does not mean that rights are reducible to duties but, rather, that rights cannot be maintained without a network of duties attached to them, some of which may be practically closer and more central to, others more distant from, the nature of each right.

Condition (3) may be met through pointing out that specific instances of pairing rights with duties and, especially, rights-bearers with rights-upholders, are frequently mistaken. Human relations are rarely diadic, and the rights–duty debate suffers from schematic oversimplification. For example, the right of a university's board of admission to refuse entry to a candidate is thought to involve no duty on the candidate's part.[48] But the duty to uphold and implement it falls on another party, namely those who have authorized the board to make the decision;[49] alternatively, that right may itself be a duty towards those keen to maintain educational standards. In other instances there may exist more than one addressee of a right or the right may be broken down into constituent parts. The right of the child to education is often paired with the duty of the parent to send it to school, rather than with the duty of a society to provide the education. It applies to both, of course.

This suggests another way of meeting condition (3). The community may itself act as intermediary between individual rights and duties. If welfare-rights may be held against a community or its agents, the duty to uphold them is communal. In legal terms this is a highly contentious position. It differs from the legal concept of rights *in rem*, because these latter liberty-rights are held potentially against anyone who might be in a position to infringe or violate them. Nor is it covered under rights *in personam*, because such claim rights require corresponding individual duty-bearers. Even a slightly extended *in personam* right only applies to a juridical person and a community is not recognized as such in law.[50]

Rights are thus both *in* a community and *of* a community. Individuals, born as they are into societies, partake by that very fact in networks of rights and duties. Initially those do not attain the status of moral imperatives but are more in the nature of existential ones. The system of mutual dependence gives rise to expectations and kinds of conduct without which human action and survival are inconceivable and that system may conveniently be described and shored up (though not solely) in terms of rights and duties. The very idea of rights and duties, it must be stressed, reflects the existence of associations between and among people. As social creatures human beings may claim rights not only against each other but against society in general, just as society will reciprocate by claiming rights against individuals.

Human rights, especially, because they are predicated on a compelling view of human functions and capacities, have general corresponding duties in a sense that rights *simpliciter* do not. But those are not rights against no one in particular. First and foremost, they are directed at the prime beneficiary of human flourishing – society itself. Indeed, the development of welfare-rights was sustained by the argument that contributions made by virtually all individuals to society justified their entitlement to communal services and goods, so that the right of the elderly to pensions, in recognition of their past labours, was a right against the community in general.[51] Of course, they are also rights against all individuals, in the sense that individuals should do their best to assist in upholding them. But it would be misleading to suggest that *all* human rights are *primarily* addressed to private individuals.

The rights *of* a community pertain to the reasonable contributions a society could exact from its members. But the peculiar nature of a community as a rights-bearer means that individuals too will benefit from the duties they discharge towards their society. And conversely, it is of great importance to re-emphasize the non-authoritarian nature of this argument, because societies only flourish insofar as their members do. Individual liberty is hence always in the social interest and its entrenched protection must be included in any formulation of the latter. The right of individuals to devise, and experiment with, their life-plans is crucial to social health as well as their own. In the ultimate analysis a society will claim duties towards itself that are shaped from a perspective broader than any individual can encompass; but it will employ those duties to ensure and augment the rights of its members. To do otherwise would be to destroy the foundations for wholesome social survival. Thus the notion of community mediates significantly between individual rights and duties, performing functions and attaining ends that individuals, utilizing private rights–duties arrangements, would be incapable of accomplishing.

What do we gain or lose from these different versions of the rights–duty complex? The choice is one between the precision of determinacy afforded by tight symmetrical theories and the flexibility and greater inclusiveness afforded by looser relationships. In the first case the notion of a right gains greater power and its implementation is more easily controlled. Individuals are locked into rigid reciprocal ties in a world that appears orderly and predictable. This is of great importance with respect to a whole range of legal rights, necessary to order the complex relationships and structures of modern societies. But legal rights are, of course, narrower as well as more specific than human rights. They will include ephemeral as well as fundamental arrangements and will be more dependent on political decisions. In the second case the notion of a right becomes a more pervasive device. Hohfeldian liberties, claims, powers and immunities will all invariably be seen as triggering behavioural reactions; the addressees of rights will be manifold, individuals as well as societies; and rights will reflect the evolution of human requirements and capacities.

Utility and Rights

One of the most lively controversies on rights in recent years has involved a debate on whether they are undermined or supported by arguments from utility. That debate interestingly illustrates some of the problems and ideological positions examined in previous chapters and has itself contributed to a closer understanding of rights-discourse. The assessment of utilitarianism from a rights-perspective has focused on important areas and occasionally opened them up to further refinement. It has allowed for a deeper inquiry into the claims of the community against the individual than is possible by means of negative-rights-theory. It has suggested ways of tackling the indefeasibility attribute of rights, endowing them – under circumscribed conditions – with the flexibility necessary for their survival and practical application. It has enabled the positioning of rights in relation to goals, to teleological views of human and social action. It has shed further light on the association of rights with well-being, benefits, needs and wants. And it has looked at the issue of the maximization of rights, and of what rights protect, under conditions of both contingent and inherent scarcity.

Classical and constrained utilitarianism

A prevalent view of utilitarianism classifies it as teleological, goal-based, maximizing; and opposes it to theories that are deontological and rights-based; indeed, that employ rights, in Nozick's phrase, as side-constraints on actions.[1] Most rights-orientated critiques of utilitarianism react to the Benthamite or classical utilitarian model. Curiously, their counter-arguments do not concentrate on that model's reductionist aspects, which depict human beings as pleasure-seeking individuals. Nor do they take undue exception to the ahistoricism that engulfs the utilitarian debate on rights. What raises their ire is a paradoxical byproduct of Bentham's strongly individualist and atomistic utilitarianism: the possibility of overriding individual goods and interests in a determination to arrive at the greatest good of the greatest number; in other words, the vulnerability of separate individuals to considerations of the general interest as well as the attenuation of the equal treatment of individuals.

Act-utilitarianism in particular has been criticized for substituting a calculus of happiness for the protection of human rights, thus severely weakening the equal respect for each individual that is considered to lie at the heart of most moral theory. Rule-utilitarianism is not regarded much more highly because of the inflexibility imposed on behaviour by the notion of a rule that is always beneficial. Some philosophers urge that rights ought to be respected for their own sake and not for any further benefit they may bring about.[2] It is, however, unclear why one can talk about a right to 'freedom or autonomy for its own sake' and yet dismiss it as a benefit by *contrasting* it with further benefits or why further benefits, such as well-being, cannot be protected for their 'own sake' as well. Such philosophers also believe that actions may be intrinsically wrong irrespective of their consequences. It remains, however, to be seen whether the types of action designated as intrinsically wrong are not, by some extraordinary 'coincidence', those that a theorist ideologically predisposed to individual autonomy, choice, and the indefeasibility of rights would select. Indeed, such moral philosophers are more prone, by the very nature of their enterprise, to seek the rigid conceptual boundaries and guidelines for conduct that elude, or are forsaken by, other rights-theorists. As we shall see, one may well hold to a temperate version of this view without abandoning all the features of utilitarianism.

 A well known critic of utilitarianism as a theory of law that excludes individual human rights, Dworkin, has offered two main criticisms which, while related, are analytically distinct. First, utilitarianism identifies the notion of average or collective welfare as the goal of human action.[3] It is, on Dworkin's understanding, 'concerned with the welfare of any particular individual only in so far as this contributes to some state of affairs stipulated as good quite apart from his choice of that state of affairs'.[4] It must therefore be constrained or, better, replaced by a rights-based theory centring on individual independence. In other words, utilitarian theories are those that, among others, can pursue human welfare without including individual independence as a facet of that welfare. Clearly, a conflict between general welfare and rights is only possible on the aggregative and exclusively quantitative notion of welfare noted in Chapter 4 or, alternatively, on Lyons's association of welfare, efficiency and utility.[5]

Second, Dworkin regards utilitarianism as revolving round the equal preferences of persons, which can then be aggregated to arrive at a binding decision. Crucially, the unit aggregated is the individual will, irrespective of its content. If, however, those aggregate wishes are used to express preference for certain people's wills – e.g. white persons (irrespective of their content) – over other persons, they will contradict the utilitarian guidelines that demand equal weighting for all in the formulation of preferences. Hence utilitarianism may be forced out of a neutral stance and bring about a situation in which someone may 'suffer disadvantage in the distribution of goods or opportunities'[6] because of the wills of others.

Here lies a division between libertarian and liberal anti-utilitarians. While the former insist on the separateness of persons and are mainly concerned with the utilitarian threat to the exercise of wide-ranging individual choice (limited only by the right of others to the same),[7] the latter are concerned with its threat to a more generously equal treatment of members of a society by its government.[8] Indeed, such opponents criticize utilitarianism for not incorporating any guarantee of the equal distribution of goods,[9] thus weakening the contrary assertion that liberalism requires the equal distribution of rights to some goods.[10] This view is asserted most strongly in current American versions of liberalism, where individuals alone are units of analysis, all persons are such units (universalism), the state is capable of neutrality with respect to the ends of its citizens, and hence equal regard for, and treatment of, persons must be upheld. To ensure this, individuals must be granted a right to moral independence as a trump over unrestricted utilitarianism.[11] In other words, utilitarian theories allow some individuals to impose their will on others – irrespective of the content of that aggregated will – thus undermining the liberal-egalitarian component Dworkin wishes to preserve.

More generally, Dworkin defines a right as a claim that it would be wrong for a government to deny an individual even if it would be in the general interest to do so.[12] Indeed, he believes the only defensible form of utilitarianism to be an egalitarian version which concentrates entirely on preferences that people express for their own good only, not for the good of others.[13] This view is acceptable only if we (1) detach important interests from rights, (2) distinguish between what is good for the generality of people and what is good for an individual, and (3) accept the proposition that neutrality with respect to what is good for individuals is both possible and desirable. Approaches such as these exclude the possibility of defining an interest so as to coincide with the preservation of fundamental rights,[14] or overlook the possibility that it may be in the general interest that the rights of all individuals be upheld and that others will act to support those rights. Dworkin opts for a classical utilitarian definition of interest, whereas other variants of utilitarianism, notably the liberal-social one, regard the notion of the general interest as necessarily attentive to individual rights. On this view the general interest can never require the overriding of a fundamental individual right. Clearly, the ambivalence attaching to the term 'interest' needs to be recognized. Finally, Dworkin propounds a specious neutrality that is not borne out by marrying rights to certain values rather than others.

The utilitarian model is employed by many scholars in an entirely ahistorical manner, without reference to the important developments it has undergone in social theory, and frequently as an Aunt Sally that may conveniently be knocked down in order to emphasize the reasonableness of antithetical notions. Frey draws attention to the fact that critics almost always attack an 'unconstrained classical utilitarianism',[15] and it is, of course, an easy target for demolition. No great powers of argument are needed to dismiss it as encouraging the defeasibility of individual rights. That unadulterated version is, however, hardly ever to be found in human action or social organization.

Alternatively, Lyons narrowly associates the human welfare to which utilitarianism appeals with economic efficiency, opposing it to the normative force of moral rights independent not only of their utility but of their enforcement and recognition.[16] Even the wider interpretation of utilitarianism as having to do with happiness and welfare, although not with purposive agency or human and social creativity, is as artificial a designation of the term as any other. Does all this warrant Hart's conclusion that '[no] satisfactory foundation for a theory of rights will be found as long as the search is conducted in the shadow of utilitarianism'?[17] As we have seen in the previous chapter, it is equally plausible to define human welfare not only in terms of pleasure widely understood but in terms of the wholesome exercise of human faculties. Welfare can quite readily encompass expressiveness and autonomy as well as enjoyment and health. Armed with Ritchie's insights discussed in Chapter 5 we may be better equipped to assess the utility/rights debate.

Frey, however, displays a philosopher's purism when he expresses concern over the introduction into utilitarianism of features that 'run against the grain of that theory'.[18] This is precisely what theorists such as Ritchie accomplished, and it also points the way to salvaging those facets of utilitarianism that may be helpfully used to bolster rights-discourse. The historical development of utilitarian thought effected compromises that may be philosophically hybrid but have nevertheless been socially and politically serviceable. Given the impossibility of constructing a wholly satisfying pure theory, the constraints of essential contestability as well as the attractions of rival social theories will occasion mutations that, while not totally operational, offer broad guidelines for action. At the same time we must reiterate that firm boundaries of categories of action, or a clear scale of options, are impossible to achieve. To that extent, politics will always remain an art, always rest in part on culturally predicated intuitions and dispositions,[19] always appeal to human 'reason' while conceding that rational unanimity is a chimera. To that extent the rigour some philosophers seek to impose on the concept of a right and its usage is bound to be frustrated. To that extent, also, the variables of rights-theory will always be open to discussion, even though a high consensus may obtain with respect to some of them.

Let us examine the questions we posed at the outset of this chapter in greater detail. The rise of the genre of social utility, envisaging a society acting to promote its specific interests, permits us at the very least to identify two units whose good requires promotion and whose rights need to be protected. This can make matters more difficult for the theorist but it can solve some problems, too. An individualistic theory of rights is quite unambiguous on the nature of the rights-bearer and can indeed allow man to be the measure of all things. A community demonstrating needs and claiming rights of its own conjures up a potentially competitive situation, in which the good, or welfare, of the one unit must be weighed against that of the other. But the result of this weighing is not a foregone conclusion, unless dubious quantitative criteria are employed. True, it may be useful for the community or its agents to deceive its members about an impending currency devaluation, even though individual rights such as free access to information, or the need for financial security, may be damaged in the process. But it may also be the case that the freedom of worship of an individual, even if costly and offensive to most members of the community, is deemed a beneficial goal that justifies the sacrifice of other goods by that majority. Ultimately the distinction may well be spurious. The right to medical care is intended to enhance individual welfare but it can simultaneously serve the communal end of a healthier, more energetic and more supportive population as part of the right of a community to ensure *its* optimal functioning. The individual and the community need not have uncontainable conflicting rights any more than two individuals in choice-rights theory will. It is always a possibility but it is very far from being a doctrinal necessity.

Critics of utilitarianism dismiss it for failing to subscribe to a concept of the person[20] as autonomous, separate, and valuable, and for implying that one person is replaceable by another. As Frey has written of the unconstrained version, 'there is no person who in principle is beyond the scope of utilitarian sacrifice.'[21] But alternative conceptions of human nature would retain the appreciation of the value of the person, and of differences among people, while regarding the person as (1) a bundle of needs and capabilities, of which autonomy is only one component; and (2) situated within a social, communitarian context. To subscribe to (1) would not diminish equal respect and concern for the rights of the individual.[22] It would mean entertaining an idea of the person in which a balance between autonomy and other attributes was attainable, inasmuch as there existed conflict among them.[23] It would enable the deployment of the broader sense of human welfare we have examined as the standard by which acts and social arrangements ought to be evaluated. It would legitimate clearly controlled external intervention in individual welfare. All these are aspects of utilitarian thought that would otherwise be tossed out with the bathwater of its unconstrained classical version. To subscribe to (2) would furthermore, as we have seen, substitute a communitarian viewpoint for an aggregative one, without denying the validity of the above elements. All this would be entirely congruent with Frey's own perception of moral rights as 'typically postulated in order to protect persons and their vital interests'.[24] It might be described as 'constrained consequentialism'.

We must now add one further dimension to the discussion. The conventional practice is to interpret utilitarianism as expressing individual, subjective preferences, albeit commensurable ones. This is a corollary of the ideological identification of the individual as the sole unit of social analysis, and of the extolling of private wills as the supreme expression of human faculties, which libertarians and many liberals endorse. Can utilitarian perspectives survive when attached to different ideological premises, held by left-liberals and many socialists, which allow for a group or a community to express their wills, even to reflect the wills of their members as part of that group-expression? Scanlon has plausibly argued that personal subjectivism is not essential to a utilitarian perspective. He contends that the criteria for evaluating consequences have to be supplied not by subjective preferences but by 'an ethically significant, objective notion of the relative importance of various benefits and burdens'.[25] However, the attainment of such objectivity may place too great a burden on its seekers. Such a recommendation would be more effective if objectivity were relinquished. Instead, one could select an alternative ideological position that introduces the preferences of groups, both in the form of their specific interests and of the interests of their members which they may occasionally (certainly not always!) be better at furthering. Individuals will not *always* act in their own best interests (although they will frequently do so), so that social decisions may replace individual choices and desires if and only if those decisions also incorporate a genuine concern for irreducible *individual* interests. There is no intrinsic reason why individuals should always pursue their own good or why they will always do so better than others can do it for them. But that crucial option must be made available for them, for they will often succeed in pursuing their own good, or at least benefit from the attempt. Its availability will depend on a set of social beliefs that sees no inevitable contradiction between group and personal values and allows for their harmonious pursuit.

The problem with common critiques of utilitarianism is that while correctly defining it as justifying actions in terms of their beneficial results they do not allow for the possibility that utilitarians may allocate some permanently good consequences to specific actions. Purists may be reluctant to call this variant 'utilitarianism' but, after all, exceptionless social theories are impossible to construct, let alone operationalize, and it is difficult to see why such stringency must be applied to utilitarianism when it can be satisfied by no other theory. What we are discussing, then, is a modified or constrained utilitarian position that, while recognizing certain goods that are either currently or permanently valuable for human beings, seeks a measure of human utility in their attainment.[26] It would seem pedantic, for example, to suggest that a utilitarian would ever wish to deny that clean air has permanently good consequences for human life. Even when we move into more complex areas of political argument, many utilitarians will regard the minimal promotion of liberty as always beneficial.[27] Moreover, welfare theorists may identify as essential some actions that lead to human flourishing; while for social utilitarians the enhancement of community life will always be a desirable and necessary yardstick of utility. The point is not that the logic of abstract utilitarianism could rule out these positions but that empirically observable political thinking displays strong utilitarian tendencies to optimize human well-being in conjunction with preserving human rights.

I have chosen the term 'optimize', not 'maximize', because on some counts the utilitarian enterprise is flawed. Utilitarians have traditionally been concerned with maximizing those features of human nature they regard as core aspects; specifically, with the human capacity for pleasure, although that has developed over time into the maximization of human desires or preferences, which Frey has termed 'interest-satisfaction'.[28] Among the criticisms of utilitarianism, three may be singled out for our purposes. First, it is often futile to calculate the quantitative benefit gained from the attainment of a good, or to calculate the amount of one good in relation to another. There are large areas of human well-being where a good must remain a question of judgement, not of measurement. Second, utilitarians who persevere in the attempt to attain the highest sum total of human happiness, even if that could only be achieved at the expense of sacrificing or seriously diminishing some important goods, are unnecessarily intransigent. Third, much utilitarianism is narrowly individualistic and subjective as it ignores the distinction between needs and wants and is concerned entirely with the latter.

Of course, maximization suggests a possible dynamic, a process, and hence utilitarians may find superficial common ground with those rights-theorists who use a related, though far from identical term – self-realization. The quantitative connotations of maximization may be at odds with the qualitative implications of self-realization; both, however, offer a purview of human nature in which certain aspects of that nature can be enhanced. What unconstrained utilitarianism lacks most blatantly in this connection is any position on the permanence of such enhancement, any notion of the continuity of the individual personality that is the object of that process. The essence of self-realization is the maturing of a potential core of attributes on a cumulative basis towards their full expression, and unconstrained utilitarianism knows nothing of all this.

The optimal result for the realization of a particular value will fall at any point between an irreducible minimum and the most that can be obtained in a concrete social and historical situation. Effectively, this means that within any set of circumstances the value should be pursued (by an individual alone, in conjunction with others, or, in rare circumstances, by others alone), without damaging other fundamental goods or values.[29] Although different desirable goals may be (partly) compatible, one has to acknowledge the conflicts that can exist among them and seek therefore to achieve those goals only up to the point where the realization of one does not *seriously* curtail the attainment of another.[30] This is feasible optimality, based on empirical possibilities of human potential and social organization. But it is not simply what *can* be achieved *now*. It is the nearest approximation to what *could* be achieved if a society were to pursue those ends wholeheartedly.

The burden placed on the word 'seriously' inevitably leads to a second sphere of value-judgements. Having stipulated the first sphere – the goods that are fundamentally desirable and worthy of rights-protection – we must assess the (possibly cultural-relative, possibly knowledge-impartial)[31] amount of each good considered to be essential. However, once we are required to weigh the attainment of (an incremental addition of) one good against (an incremental addition of) another, decisions become increasingly arbitrary, because we are dealing with incommensurable goods and values. As Griffin puts it, incommensurability entails that 'no amount of [one value] could outweigh a certain amount of the other.'[32] In rights-respecting societies, the identification of that 'certain amount' lies at the heart of political argument over rights.

The limits of trade offs and competition

The above discussion bears on the complicated issue of trade offs between values. Trade offs are a particular instance of the economic scarcity problem. If you cannot have enough of good A and good B concurrently, and yet want both, you will have to make an (ideological) decision about how much of each to demand and how much of one good you are prepared to purchase by diminishing the other. The existence of scarce goods necessitates important decisions on distribution, whereas the insistence on the *right* to a good ensures that *some* of it will be available to any rights-bearer. Otherwise, the concept as well as the practice of rights could be undermined by trade offs which reduce them to 'mere shadows' or 'appendages',[33] especially when they are used to choose between the goods of different people in order to maximize an aggregate good. Any discussion must consider the following points.

(1) On one view (1.1) some goods are essential to human welfare so that the more there is of them the better – they should be maximized. Health and education are examples. Both are not *inherently* scarce goods because the maximization of the good for one individual does not rule out its maximization for another. Although practically a society may not be able to give me all the education I need in order to be an autonomous creature, my right to it still exists, even if unrealized. But on another view (1.2) the incremental utility of such goods may decrease as we move further in the direction of their maximization or, more simply, they may become less crucial to human functioning. So while it is nice to have the right to everything that my health requires, it is more important to have the right to what will keep me alive than to what will make me a great athlete. On this interpretation the strong right to some goods will weaken on a continuum; after all, there are limits on the available means to attaining them. Consequently we may establish a pecking order of the rights to different goods that are conducive to health, reflecting their qualitative variations. In that weaker area

alone, further down the ranking order, trade offs among goods may be legitimate. But even then, there is no trade off between the rights to health and education, as clarified in (5) below.

(2) Some goods are essential to human welfare, but plainly not in maximized quantity. Choice may be considered necessary to human well-being, but unlimited choice is not. As we have seen in Chapter 4, the simplistic yet common view that the more choice the better does not stand up to serious scrutiny. It would only hold true on the assumption of full human rationality. Although the act of choosing may be what makes a person a rational being and is essential to the development of human capacities,[34] people are quite capable of making choices that damage, endanger or dehumanize them. Whether they should have the right to such choice is debatable, if a right denotes the protection of something of value.[35]

Likewise, the suggestion that property is vital for the realization of personality does not mean that all property, or superabundant property, is. The right to such goods[36] could be restricted for the following reasons. First, some forms of them may be harmful, as in the case of choice. Second, a good may be contingently scarce, as in the case of most material objects. Third, the indiscriminate pursuit of any category of goods may be impossible without diminishing the availability of another valued category to which people have a right (e.g. liberty–property). The pursuit of liberty, for example, may also curtail the availability of goods of type (1.1), which can be maximized without restriction. For instance, my liberty may include the liberty *not* to cater for my health and education. In sum, rights can protect values only within a range that is not permitted to be *either* minimizable *or* maximizable.[37]

This analysis also has important implications for the preference issue. While it is well understood, for example, that free speech may be crucial to social well-being, the complementary principle – that some types of free speech are inimical to well-being – is frequently ignored, not only by straightforward libertarians but by more sophisticated theorists. Campbell is too prone to take classical utilitarianism at face value, dismissing it because 'when utility is measured in terms of individual preferences it gives equal weight to all preferences or satisfactions.' However, the decoding of classical utilitarianism reveals again that the choice/individualist model, like any ideological position, favours certain types of human activity and concern. Campbell is therefore wrong in suggesting that socialism is

unique in valuing 'certain types of human activity and concern above others'.[38]

(3) So far we have been talking about trade offs among goods or values. But there may also be trade offs among rights themselves. For instance, the optionalizing of rights makes them potentially scarce – some may waive them, others not; some rights may be alienable, others not. Hence some individuals will bear such rights; others will not. Here we can envisage the purchase of rights, the currency being another right or a different good. If you accord me the right to walk through your garden, I will give you the right to use my car. Less trivial trade offs in the form of negative purchases could also be theoretically possible: if the government waives its right to extract military service from me, I will waive my right to claim welfare benefits. Alternatively I could purchase the (immunity) right to exemption from such service by paying a large sum of money. Of course, if rights are meant to protect necessary benefits, this optional trading would be illegitimate because it would deny both the individual and the community vital goods.

(4) The specific attributes of a right may also be scarce. There may be a problem of competition over the degree of *protection* afforded by a right. If absoluteness is the attribute of a right it will, as we have seen in Chapter 3, create scarcity among other rights, for the absolute protection of all competing values by rights is impossible. We are contemplating here not the availability of a good but the indefeasibility of a right. If all rights are indefeasible, some *rights*, and not only *goods*, will compete with others. Hence rights, if they offer too strong protection, can suffer from intrinsic scarcity.

(5) Trade offs among rights are further possible because a right is a *prioritizing* device, and there will be a scarcity of preferred positions on a scale of rights. One way of coping with this competitive situation is to eliminate one of the competing rights. Thus those who claim that the right to choice is limited by the right to physical welfare may deny the one or the other the status of a right. People will therefore compete over what merits the status of a right, and they will then further compete over the priority of such assignments. The alternative, as suggested in Chapter 4, is to treat basic human rights as indivisible. That indivisibility relates to the interlinked categories of physical, mental, psychological and moral attributes, each of which demands equal consideration, so that a

trade off between, say, the right to liberty and to health (as unconstrained utilitarians might propose) is ruled out.

But *within* each category there will be more important and less important requirements, enabling rights to be ranked. Free speech may be more important than free consumer choice in the category of moral autonomy. Food may be more important than unpolluted air in the category of physical needs. But free speech is incommensurable with food, and consumer choice with unpolluted air, because they inhabit different categories. Rights are about prioritizing but they are also about protecting *all* areas considered essential to human flourishing. Trade offs are then restricted either to some derivative or optional rights or, as we saw in (1) above, apply not to the *right* but to the *quantity of the good* (1.1) or to the *lower quality goods* (1.2) the right protects. Because of the incommensurability problem, maximization is replaced by optimization.[39]

On the multi-dimensional model of human nature equal status is accorded to a range of human faculties. Rights will have been chosen in such a way as to minimize competition *between* faculty and faculty, to avoid the eventuality by which the realization of one faculty diminishes the realization of another, whether of the same or of another person. The pegging of either the quantity or the quality of the protected good is another decision that reflects variable human conventions and ideologies. If we aim for a standard of adequate human functioning we may wish to set our sights lower than if we aim for the more generous standard of human flourishing. It is vital, however, that a core of each and every identified good be secured for the members of a society as a matter of right. Trade offs should, ideally, only be entered into outside that area.

Another way of putting the general issue is to assign lexical priority to the securing of basic human goods over the maximizing aspect of the utility principle.[40] Although philosophers and lawyers frequently seek to establish clear boundaries beyond which the pursuit of a right becomes logically or legally unsustainable, those boundaries are flexible. They are the product of moral principles and cultural norms which are constantly subject to reassessment on the basis of new scientific knowledge, e.g. on the question of when does life begin, or what are necessary ecological requirements, as well as on the basis of refinements and changes in moral climates. This is in the very nature of concrete rights-debates; they cannot be contained within rigid conceptual and theoretical guidelines precisely because human understanding is continuously restructuring the frameworks to which those guidelines refer.

So far we have been deliberating the trade offs among rights and between rights and utility. There is another major area that still merits separate consideration: the balance between the concept of rights and other central political concepts such as the public interest, equality or power. It could, of course, be suggested that by defining a right as a special device according protection to values we have already allowed rights to override other, unprotected, values. Nevertheless, this is too simplistic. Some values stand on their own without needing the protection of rights. At best they can then be formulated as second order rights. The objective of economic self-sufficiency may appear valuable but can hardly be claimed as a right, other than the second order right of elected governments to make decisions on behalf of their citizens.

We must hence confront some confusing issues. Is government censorship, when directed against the publication of allegedly sensitive material, an example of competition between the public interest and the right to freedom of expression? Is the need for affirmative action to increase the life chances of underprivileged minorities an example of competition between an imposed equality of opportunity and the equal rights of individuals to the same treatment? Is the requirement to preserve the monopoly of trade unions as representatives of workers' interests an example of competition between the felicitous power of groups and the rights of individuals to choose their association?

Exploring the possibilities of acceptable trade offs between these conflicting values highlights not only the difficulty of balancing different justifiable viewpoints, but also the multiple meanings any of these concepts can carry. In Chapter 1 the structures of various ideologies, as diverse configurations of concepts, was discussed. Conservatives, liberals and socialists all subscribe to a concept of rights, but each will surround their respective concept with different adjacent concepts that will inform and colour the meaning of the term 'rights' within each ideology.

To illustrate briefly: because conservatives tend to understand rights within the framework of custom, authority and respect for formal legal arrangements, because they prefer to talk about states and nations rather than communities, the adjacent concept of 'public interest' will be defined and handed down by authoritative state agencies such as governments, denied more than one interpretation and allowed to override individual rights that challenge it. Indeed, the state, in defining *its* interest, may abrogate those rights. In contrast a classical liberal interpretation, stressing individual self-determination and the accountability and limits of state power, may see the 'public interest' *as* the defence of private rights against the superimposition of interests external to and unwanted by individuals.

A third possibility attaches the public interest to a more generous definition of 'public', construed as pertaining to community interests, sometimes in harmony and sometimes conflicting with individual interests and rights. Socialists may regard the right to work as involving community provision of work and the drafting of resources to that effect. The community interest will lie in cultivating natural human productivity and creativity as well as in the security deriving from regular and sufficient remuneration. It will also encourage the satisfaction and hence greater capacity for active citizenship of its members, although some non-socialists will feel that it is against their interests to subsidize those who have failed to compete in the marketplace, and that the latter are responsible for their own failure. Conservatives, who view individual rights within a self-balancing social order, and regard excessive intervention in individual chances as both unjust and socially destabilizing, may object to any extension of the right to subsistence into the field of labour, except to maintain freedom of choice with regard to an occupation and to lift the barriers to the smooth operation of a free market.

Socialists may see trade union organization as the only hope for redressing the domination and exploitation of the working class, and hence protect that countervailing power through group-rights-language, but liberals may regard power as inherently threatening unless diffused via a one-person, one-vote democratic process. The permutations are legion, but two rules remain. First, our understanding of rights depends on the conceptual environment in which competing ideologies situate them. Second, the concept of rights may be stretched or contracted, to include or to oppose other basic political concepts. Likewise, other concepts may be expanded to coincide with rights or constricted to exclude them.

Assessing modified utilitarianism

Three conclusions derive from the above. First, a modified, constrained utilitarianism will dissociate itself from classical act- and rule-utilitarianism, retaining instead a commitment to those acts and rules that are conducive to the values held to be humanly pertinent and socially desirable. Whether or not these are time- and culture-specific is a secondary issue. The proviso must be added that such rules be subject to adaptation – not to petty quantitative calculations but to reasoned changes in moral stances and empirical knowledge. Second, a social-utilitarian perspective can combine the protection and encouragement of individual flourishing with the preservation of social interests, because it assumes that, prima-facie, the promotion of human rights that ensure such flourishing *is* conducive to the general welfare.[41] The borderline cases of conflict between human rights and general welfare that nevertheless still exist are the bane that any non-utopian or perfectionist political concept must necessarily endure. The fact that they are not neatly soluble should not deter us from an effort to tidy up the main spread of the concept. The contrary belief that they *are* soluble is all too frequently productive of bad theory. Third, a modified utilitarianism will attach significance to the role of individual wills in contributing towards the articulation of basic interests. It will crucially retain an interest in the plurality of individual lives and in the utility of the right to a generous range of forms of self-expression.

A rights-supportive modified utilitarianism would have to be superimposed on and secondary to certain socio-ethical prerequisites which concern the desirability of human flourishing and which accept that healthy communities are composed of, and dependent on, the welfare of all their members and the attainment of irreducible minima of welfare for each. This is precisely the cut off point the absence of which in unconstrained utilitarianism is bemoaned by Frey.[42] Another way of looking at the problem is to limit the divergence between goal-based and right-based principles[43] by suggesting that one kind of goal-based theory will include as a central goal the protection of those attributes that right-based theories deem precious. As we have seen, the distinction between goal-based and rights-based theories obfuscates the prior dependence of both on ethical and ideological assumptions that determine what the goals or rights are.

Rather than regarding basic human rights as axiomatic,[44] or natural, the modified utilitarian approach prefers to present them as reflecting significantly useful cultural assumptions (irrespective of their truth) made in order to secure arrangements congenial to social organization.[45] Indeed, Mackie has adumbrated a process of moral thinking that 'would work up from below', from negotiation and debate among conflicting views and claims (although he tends to see these as conscious and deliberate transactions rather than semi-haphazard occurrences within a historical timespan). In so doing he usefully detaches the philosopher from a supra-conflictual position to no more than an articulate representative of human viewpoints, subject to the same historical and social forces as all members of a society. He refers promisingly to a 'utilitarianism of rights' that could handle conflicts among prima-facie rights.[46] On closer inspection, however, it involves maximizing the total rights-fulfilment of members of a society and minimizing their total rights-infringement. Hence this proposal, too, fails to meet the requirements of a modified utilitarianism because it persists in ignoring both the importance of the individual as the unit of analysis and the bottom line beneath which the dehumanization of such individuals would commence.

Instead, Mackie expresses a curious preference for a compromise formula that would, when conflict among rights arose, infringe all people's rights equally and therefore dehumanize them all. Not all equal treatment is *ipso facto* fair treatment: a tyrant may boil all his subjects in oil. It could of course be argued that the equal diminishing of rights is legitimate if all those involved voluntarily submit to it. The availability of such consent is predicated on the choice-theory of right, which in its strong version allows individuals to will away their rights to the point of their own dehumanization, and denies them rights against themselves. McCloskey, however, suggests that another connection between rights and utility is possible in one respect:

> a *prima facie* rights-theory would have no affinities at all with [unconstrained] utilitarianism other than having a maximizing calculus. However, it would be a calculus about maximizing satisfaction of rights and only that.[47]

Unfortunately he does not pursue this vital and perfectly workable overlap between the two approaches.

Ultimately, our understanding of human nature, its needs and capacities, within a social context, provides the 'argumentative threshold'[48] that gives a human-rights theory its force. It is not an unconstrained utilitarian argument about maximizing the general welfare but one about optimizing currently available and persuasive conceptions of human functioning.

Human Rights in Practice: A Sampling of Problems

In examining the general case for an extended view of human rights a three-dimensional model of rights has been proposed, incorporating the equal weighting and indivisibility of fundamental human attributes, the communal nature of human beings and their inherent developmentalism. The abandonment of fixed lists is a necessary consequence of this latter characteristic. Instead, a notion of flexible rights-clusters may be employed, in conjunction with the strategy, examined in Chapter 6, that aims at a sustainable level for every attribute that the various rights in the cluster protect or enable.

But what rights should people actually have? And how would they relate to contemporary programmes such as the main declarations sponsored by international agencies and organizations or to civil rights and liberties questions? This book ends by way of a brief survey and necessarily illustrative analysis of the problems and issues addressed by contemporary rights-debates.

Formal statements

Too many modern constitutions incorporating Bills of Rights or their equivalent exist to be discussed here; but the past half-century has seen a number of significant supranational pronouncements. Among them the Universal Declaration of Human Rights (1948) has rightly been singled out as the most important and influential twentieth-century document. It has also been accused of being a repository of Western political thinking, which undermines its universal aspirations, and defended from that accusation. To assess its ideological status, and to understand the evolution of rights-debate in the second half of this century, it would be useful to examine some of its principles as they compare with later documents. The Declaration certainly reasserts the conventional rights of individuals in the Western tradition: life, liberty, security of person, equality of dignity, the application of equal and fair legal procedures, freedom of opinion, of expression, of association and of representation. But it also contains rights that twentieth-century sensibilities have become particularly attuned to: protection against torture or cruel, inhuman or degrading treatment or punishment; freedom of movement in and out of a state; freedom of asylum from persecution. Such rights are based on a wider purview of the prerequisites for human welfare, on physical and psychological as well as mental and moral requirements. In addition to those civil and political rights, the Declaration comprises what are known as second generation rights: economic, social and cultural rights such as those to food, clothing, housing and health, to social security, to work, to just and favourable remuneration, to rest and leisure, to membership of trade unions and to education. Mothers and children are accorded specific human rights.

Most of the above rights could secure general approval, although even then trade union rights in particular and the extent of second generation rights in general would not satisfy all ideological positions. But it is an overstatement to describe them as 'the world's first universal ideology'.[1] Any right may be the subject of varying interpretations by its endorsers. Furthermore, there are explicit and implicit assumptions in the Declaration that indicate the changing and occasionally tentative nature of some of its tenets. The right to property has been notably downgraded in this and other modern documents, moving well down the list of essentials; yet a thoroughly capitalist principle – the right to the protection of material interests resulting from scientific, literary or artistic productions (in other words, copyright) – has been entrenched. The designation of the family as 'the natural and fundamental group unit of society' points both to the perceived universal permanence of that institution, communist and anarchist experiments to the contrary, and to the incipient recognition of groups as empirical and analytical constructs. Education is linked to 'the full development of the human personality' and that development is significantly attached to community membership through the assignment of duties: 'Everyone has duties to the community in which alone the free and full development of his personality is possible.' Finally, by securing all the rights and freedoms of the Declaration on equal footing, the third dimension of contemporary rights-discourse – their indivisibility – is established.

While some scholars support this disinclination to rank rights[2] Nickel, who contends that some rights are weightier than others, sees it as a weakness.[3] True, some documents, for instance the International Covenant on Civil and Political Rights (CPR) (1966), distinguish between derogable and non-derogable rights; but this distinction could equally be grounded on the difference between rights that are more immediately implementable and those requiring a programme of progressive realization over time;[4] or on the difference between rights that have reasonably clear cores and boundaries (such as the right not to be subject to the deliberate infliction of pain) and those whose core is surrounded by a broad grey area that permits a degree of leeway before they are intolerably violated (such as the right to education).[5] In principle, with the exception of the abstract right to exist, the ranking of basic rights is difficult to uphold; but in practice there may be greater urgency in upholding some rights rather than others: the right not to suffer torture in an unsavoury dictatorship, the right to nutrition in a drought-ridden country, the right to types of welfare and social assistance in a number of capitalist systems. If at all, this reinforces a culturally relative rather than universal and intrinsic basis for ranking rights; otherwise, the only permissible rankings are those discussed in Chapter 6.

Many of the above rights are derivative from one another. The right to life, for example, has been historically extended from protection against arbitrary killing, through including the servicing of attributes without which human existence is impossible (food, shelter, clothing), to encompassing dignified human life (by means of work and adequate remuneration, without which human life is substandard) and finally, to full human expression and development (without which human life is impoverished or unrealized). In each category there is, of course, room for much ideological negotiation; the American Convention on Human Rights (1969), for example, defines life controversially as beginning 'from the moment of conception'.

Later documents expand on some of these themes and also

introduce a few new additions.[6] One such addition concerns the thorny problem of the limitations that can be put on the claiming of rights and employs two strategies. The first pertains to the contentious content of one of the most fundamental need-related rights, the right to health. The International Covenant on Economic, Social and Cultural Rights (ESCR) (1966) recognizes 'the right of everyone to the enjoyment of the highest attainable standard of physical and mental health' (similar language was used by the European Social Charter (1961)). This surpasses the notion of 'adequacy' of the 1948 Declaration, clearly avoids any limitation of that right on grounds of competing claims, needs or interests and presents it as an open-ended commitment, subject only to what can be achieved at the time. Such a maximizing formulation of an 'insatiable' right is bound to worry negative- and forbearance-rights-theorists.

The second strategy accepts the limitation of some rights by the 'rights and freedoms of others' as well as by competing values, such as national security, public health or morals, or public order. But whereas public order or safety relate to the observance of non-violent and orderly behaviour, the European Charter and the earlier European Convention for the Protection of Human Rights and Fundamental Freedoms (1950) employ the term 'public interest', a much wider and more malleable phrase that can give succour to many governmental activities. In view of that vagueness it is particularly important that further provisos are added restricting such limitations 'solely for the purpose of promoting the general welfare in a democratic society' (ESCR, article 4, and similarly for the American continent in the American Convention, although also in the American Declaration that preceded the Universal Declaration by a day). Written niceties, however, do not always reflect political and social realities. The West European record on human rights is better, with some notable exceptions, than that of many Central and South American countries.

Property rights undergo further attenuation. The 1966 Covenants fail to mention them altogether. The European Convention invokes the public interest in order to permit divesting individuals of their possessions. The American Declaration made an early stand on a minimalist approach to property, establishing a right only to 'own such private property as meets the essential needs of decent living', and the American Convention subordinated the use and enjoyment of individual property to the interest of society or public utility.

On the other hand, the rights of groups, sometimes termed third generation rights, receive greater airing. The right of peoples to self-determination has been joined in the African Charter on Human and People's Rights (1981) by the right to development, and more recently – in 1986 – by the Declaration on the Right to Development of the General Assembly of the United Nations, pertaining to individuals and peoples.[7] Indeed, the right to development is expressed in increasingly emphatic language. The African Charter asserts that 'States shall have the duty, individually or collectively, to ensure the exercise of the right to development' (article 22), and a draft Convention on the Rights of the Child refers to 'the promotion of the development of the child's personality, talents and mental and physical abilities to their fullest potential'.[8]

Although no document is prepared to refer to the *rights* of the community, many refer to the duties and responsibilities of individuals not only towards other individuals but towards distinct entities such as the family, the community and even mankind. This is particularly pronounced in the African Charter and, of course, central to state constitutions such as the 1977 Soviet constitution. While modern documents – the American Declaration is one – imply that rights involve duties on the part of rights-bearers, they are more obscure on the question of strict correlative rights and duties. As for the issue of parallel community and individual rights, modern documents reflect the same hesitations that discussants of children's rights experienced a century ago, when they gingerly conducted their arguments by invoking duties towards children without inferring the corresponding rights that children are now considered to have.[9]

Issues

The heightened awareness of human rights has led to activity on a large number of national and international concerns. A few salient themes must suffice as concrete examples of some of the issues raised in this book. Civil liberties, asserted mainly against overbearing state regulation and intervention, are one such instance. Questions such as conscientious objection to military service have exercised individuals and governments for most of this century and the legitimation of this and other forms of civil disobedience has been increasingly demanded by those opposing governmental

action on ethical grounds. In the United States the refusal to serve
in Vietnam propelled the problem into the centre of public
attention; in Britain there have been lesser manifestations, such as
the objection by the Greenham Common women and others to
foreign missiles on British soil. The right to disobey a technically
legal command thought to be immoral or illegitimate, has been
claimed from ancient times and then preserved through the
mediaeval right to resist unlawful rulers. It has never been truly
conceded by governments, unwilling to undermine their support on
a particular policy, or to encourage a domino effect of opting out of
legal duties. But it has more recently been conceded *de facto* in
areas in which individuals may have good reasons for disobedience,
in which – unlike criminals – they appeal to alternative legitimation
and on condition that they still must, in order to maintain their
credibility and pass a 'test' of serious intentions, display obligation
towards other laws and regulations, including accepting reasonable
punishments allotted to civil disobedients.[10]

This is perhaps the most contentious area of traditional civil rights
but others abound. Lord Scarman has observed that 'human rights',
unlike 'civil liberties' is not a term of art in English law.[11] Yet many
scholars – and indeed some declarations of human rights – talk of
liberty and rights in the same breath. Historically, rights developed
as liberties against tyrannical actions of rulers[12] and referred, as we
have noted, to the creation of spaces round individuals. The
emergence of a disjuncture between liberties and rights was an
important step in the crystallization of separate conceptual identi-
ties for both terms, especially in view of the etymological relationship between liberties and liberty. Many human rights will remain
liber*ties* but the two are not collapsible into one nor is liberty (in the
singular) identical to a right or a subset of a right.

The residual nature of personal freedom in Britain has been
frequently noted. A right exists when there is a law establishing it; a
liberty when there is no law.[13] In the absence of a boundary for a
liberty British governments can, and do, use considerable powers in
controlling civil liberties and encroaching upon them. In particular,
the tricky notion of the public interest resurfaces frequently to
curtail serious challenges not only to public order but, as in the case
of the 1984 miners' strike, to the authority and policies of the
government as buttressed by police powers. Other recent British
examples are the attempts of the government to prevent the

publication of the memoirs of a former MI5 agent or the prompt governmental action over the leaking by a civil servant of documents relating to the British sinking of an Argentinian ship during the Falklands war. These reveal a growing divide between British and American practice on freedom of information and expression, exemplified by the US Supreme Court's decision on the publication of the Pentagon Papers.[14] The issue is not that the government is trespassing on forbidden ground but rather that the accommodation of the legitimate rights-protected interests of individual and community is slanted in favour of too partisan a political interpretation of that balance. Bills of Rights, however imperfect, rein in some of the slack of governmental discretion.

An entirely different area is that of women's rights, especially in Western countries where public sensibilities and women's movements have focused attention on the issue. Following on the relatively successful attainment by Western women of political rights during the past century, the general question of women's rights now has three aspects. The first simply runs as follows. Women are human beings. If human beings have rights, so do women. All the rights that human beings have apply therefore to women as to any other subcategory of human beings. This universal, abstract statement is nevertheless insufficient. It requires a second, supplementary, assertion: women have specific needs and capabilities, arising from characteristics concerning them alone, that require protection by means of rights and without which they are fundamentally dehumanized.[15] This refers to the biological and psychological complex that surrounds childbirth and mothering.[16] But there is a further, non-biological reason why women could claim specific rights. The vast majority of present social arrangements, all over the world, assign them the tasks of child care and home work. There is nothing inevitable or biologically determined about this. It is a culture-specific feature that happens to be almost universal. This central reality of women's lives justifies additional sets of rights that protect them in the 'private domain'[17] (although in some cultures women do not desire equal status with men in this sphere). The third aspect may entitle women to compensatory rights, relating to injustices done to them in the past as a group, deliberately or otherwise, the result of which is to discriminate against them, either in the eyes of the law or in actual social practice, and to make them vulnerable in a number of areas: work and wages, susceptibility to violence or harassment, unequal status with men. Those are temporary rights, the object of which is to repair a social defect and to enable women to function fully in the future.

This brings us to the issue of discrimination in general and to the affirmative action sometimes employed to counter it. Supporters of affirmative action may attempt to promote the right to equal treatment of a group at the partial expense of individuals and groups outside it, but will present this as compensation for the inadequacies of past treatment of that group, and as beneficial for the community at large. This may be seen by others as unjustified preferential treatment. The problem relates to different conceptions of equality that require rights-protection. We can regard society as a collection of persons, each meriting equal consideration. But this conception competes with an acknowledgement of further factors, such as the unequal distribution of power, that undermine that formal and minimalist equality. The consequence is a split among those advocates of civil rights and liberties who see them as a precondition for the development of individual personality alone, and those who see their function also in the redistribution of power.[18] Because power is not only a threatening but an enabling attribute, groups who have special ends they wish to promote need the right to accumulate the power necessary to those purposes. Affirmative action seeks to ensure that distribution. Nevertheless, 'innocent' contemporary individuals will be deprived of social goods for reasons beyond their responsibility. The assertion of rights may be coupled with competition over finite goods considered essential to human flourishing, such as the limited access to higher education highlighted by the Bakke case, in which an individual explained away his non-selection by a university as the result of an affirmative-action quota.[19] All attempts to reconcile the individual right to education with the group right to equal opportunity with other groups will result in essentially contestable decisions. The acceptability of anti-discrimination policies will therefore depend on the different configurations of concepts that encircle rights and liberties and give them particular ideological shape.

The issue at stake is not only that of justice for deprived individuals but the recognition of special group rights which may not be as transient as, arguably, compensatory rights for women should be. The formal equality position does not recognize the claims of groups at all. Affirmative action, however, is only a first step in recognizing special cultural (rather than racial or sexual) features that some groups have and, crucially, aspire to retain. A distinctive type of minority, which wields significant impact on the self-identity of its members, may claim the group right to cultural self-determination.[20] Cultural pluralism, group rights and the general end of preserving the basic attributes of each human being combine here to underpin a strong case for securing specific as well as universal rights. In addition to the rights of ethnic minorities the rights of indigenous peoples have been recently acknowledged.[21] In contrast, the rights of trade unions, another well aired contemporary issue, are not to be understood primarily as group rights in the above senses. They are a twentieth-century manifestation of the civil right to free association and its reasonable or unreasonable curbing when vital political, military and economic interests are at stake. This also concerns the rights of workers not to join an association in the face of trade union insistence.

Public policy-making bodies need general guidelines concerning rights that ensure they do not seriously infringe any of the basic components of human well-being. This will normally apply to run of the mill cases, such as securing people against unlawful violence, or ensuring that individuals do not die of starvation when sufficient food is available, or protecting them against arbitrary discrimination by public authorities; and it is important that those authorities, occupied as they are with large numbers of individuals, are possessed of run of the mill criteria for the manageable problems they encounter. Even so, some cases in which 'the suggested rights are basic, though defeasible'[22] may not allow for the retention of basic minima of all aspects of human well-being. These will be exceptional, but possibly important, test cases for new guidelines. Philosophers, of course, are frequently concerned with these eccentric (off centre) problems; indeed, they often conjure up hypothetical worst-case examples to frustrate the workings of any particular approach. Although such examples may discredit the general principle of protecting an irreducible minimum of desirable human capabilities and attributes, they should not discourage the formulation of run of the mill analysis to direct practical public conduct.

On many issues it is theoretically impossible to answer conclusively the question, 'does X have a right?'. Do I have, for example, a right to medical assistance as the result of a disease brought about by smoking if I have previously been warned of the consequences of that practice? An affirmative answer suggests that human beings have general claims to well-being that confer duties on any other person able to help in sustaining that well-being. Even if I alone am responsible for my condition, my co-human beings are responsible for minimizing my avoidable suffering; i.e. we are locked into a web of community obligations. A negative answer suggests that though I am free to make choices detrimental to myself, for which only I am responsible, my membership of a society does not entitle me to unmerited assistance; consequently, a society is projected in which individuals may go about their own business without owing me active duties of assistance. The theoretical impossibility of solving these issues is in inverted ratio to the practical solutions they embrace. In actual situations, rights are always either accorded or not: the hospital will either attend or not attend to me; my right will have been upheld, denied or violated. Which of these will obtain is a question of the ideological framework applied.

Because these contradictions have no intrinsic solutions, as is also the case with other key political concepts, the political system is the institution entrusted with resolving, or ideologically decontesting – at least fleetingly – areas of rights-conflict. The acceptability of its decisions will depend on the degree of democratic accountability it exhibits and on its own sensitivity to rights issues. Be that as it may, political decisions on rights-conflicts are resolutions of concrete social issues and they leave many essential rights-problems un-touched.

*   *   *

In this book I have attempted to assess the ideological implications of current rights-theories. Because of the preponderance of the individualist approach to rights, a considerable amount of space has been devoted to present alternative viewpoints. Nevertheless, rights are compatible with conservative, liberal and socialist perspectives. Given *any* set of reasonable assumptions about human nature and social structure, a serious rights-theory may be constructed and promoted. Like any rights-analyst I cannot dis-sociate myself from my own ideological preferences. But I hope to have shown that by reconsidering some traditional dichotomies –

choice/welfare, negative/positive, individual/community – a plausible basis for a humanistic rights-theory may be attained by cutting across and integrating different ideological positions.

Notes

Chapter 1

1 'Whatever rights may be, everyone agrees that they . . . are normatively advantageous.' L. W. Sumner, *The Moral Foundation of Rights* (Oxford: Oxford University Press, 1989), p. 32.

2 Aside from the centrality accorded to this document in current thinking about the effect of the revolution the title draws attention to a possible distinction between men and citizens.

3 Leo Strauss's reconstruction of the classical position – the search for truth and knowledge – in *Natural Right and History* (Chicago: Chicago University Press, 1953) is a good example of this genre, to which we shall return.

4 For a thoughtful adumbration of such intricacies see J. J. Thomson, *Rights, Restitution and Risk* (Cambridge, MA: Harvard University Press, 1986).

5 An implied, though not explicitly stated, message in A. R. White, *Rights* (Oxford: Oxford University Press, 1984), which explores the concrete relationships between rights and supportive concepts.

6 Cf. A. Gewirth, 'The Epistemology of Human Rights', *Social Philosophy and Policy*, Vol. 1 (1984), p. 10.

7 W. N. Hohfeld, *Fundamental Legal Conceptions* (New Haven: Yale University Press, 1919).

8 See C. Wellman, 'A New Conception of Human Rights' in E. Kamenka and A. E.-S. Tay, eds, *Human Rights* (London: Edward Arnold, 1978), who also attempts to extend the Hohfeldian analysis to non-legal rights.

9 C. Fried, 'Rights and the Common Law' in R. G. Frey, ed., *Utility and Rights* (Oxford: Basil Blackwell, 1985), p. 231.

10 T. Campbell, *The Left and Rights* (London: Routledge and Kegan Paul, 1983), p. 31.

11 J. Kleinig, 'Human Rights, Legal Rights and Social Change' in Kamenka and Tay, *Human Rights*, p. 46.

12 Campbell holds that only positive rights can be discussed descriptively (*The Left and Rights*, pp. 23–5). But it is equally possible, and equally important, to engage in a second order description of moral rights without entering into an ethical debate.

13 See W. Gallie, 'Essentially Contested Concepts', *Proceedings of the Aristotelian Society*, Vol. 56 (1955–6), pp. 167–98.

14 A. Gewirth, 'A Reply to Danto', *Social Philosophy and Policy*, Vol. 1 (1984), p. 31; S. Benn, 'Human Rights – for Whom and for What?' in Kamenka and Tay, *Human Rights* (London: Edward Arnold, 1978), p. 66.

15 C. R. Beitz, 'Difficulties with Flathman's Moderation Thesis', *Social Philosophy and Policy*, Vol. 1 (1984), p. 172.

16 H. J. McCloskey, 'Rights – Some Conceptual Issues', *Australasian Journal of Philosophy*, Vol. 54 (1976), p. 99.

17 N. MacCormick, *Legal Right and Social Democracy* (Oxford: Oxford University Press, 1982), p. 143.

18 J. Feinberg, *Rights, Justice and the Bounds of Liberty* (Princeton: Princeton University Press, 1980), p. 239; A. R. White, *Rights* (Oxford: Oxford University Press, 1984), p. 17.

19 See J. W. Nickel, *Making Sense of Human Rights* (Berkeley and Los Angeles: University of California Press, 1987), p. 13.

20 For culture-relativism see Chapter 3. 'Knowledge-impartial' implies correspondence with current scientific and scholarly (*wissenschaftlich*) knowledge, which claims impartiality but falls short of an absolute standard. Medicine and psychology are typical examples, but so are some branches of philosophy.

21 The practical failure to implement a right does not necessarily denote its invalidation; otherwise rights could be eliminated simply by infringing them.

22 See also White, *Rights*, pp. 172–3. By 'conventional' I do not mean sanctioned by custom, but artificially contrived.

23 See A. I. Melden, *Rights and Right Conduct* (Oxford: Basil Blackwell, 1959); M. P. Golding, 'The Concept of Rights: A Historical Sketch' in E. L. and B. Bandman, eds, *Bioethics and Human Rights* (Boston: Little, Brown, 1978), pp. 44–50; J. Donnelly, *The Concept of Human Rights* (London: Croom Helm, 1985), pp. 1–10. Alternatively, J. Rawls's conception of the right preceding the good (in *A Theory of Justice* (Oxford: Oxford University Press, 1972)) stresses its procedural characteristics.

24 See J. Finnis, *Natural Law and Natural Rights* (Oxford: Oxford University Press, 1980), pp. 92–5.

25 On this latter point see M. P. Golding, 'Towards a Theory of Human Rights', *Monist*, Vol. 52 (1968), pp. 544–5.

26 Campbell, *The Left and Rights*, p. 113.

27 See M. P. Golding, 'From Prudence to Rights: A Critique' in J. R. Pennock and J. W. Chapman, eds, *Nomos XXIII: Human Rights* (New York: New York University Press, 1981), pp. 166–9.

Chapter 2

1 See C. B. Macpherson, 'Natural Rights in Hobbes and Locke' in D. D. Raphael, ed., *Political Theory and the Rights of Man* (London: Macmillan, 1967), p. 4.
2 Cf. I. Shapiro, *The Evolution of Rights in Liberal Theory* (Cambridge: Cambridge University Press, 1986), p. 41.
3 T. Hobbes, *Leviathan* (Harmondsworth: Penguin, 1968), p. 189.
4 Ibid., p. 191.
5 Ibid.
6 Ibid., pp. 192, 227.
7 J. Finnis, *Natural Law and Natural Rights* (Oxford: Oxford University Press, 1980), p. 208.
8 Hobbes, *Leviathan*, p. 191.
9 For a useful analysis of the ideological assumptions implicit in Hobbes's views see Shapiro, *The Evolution of Rights*.
10 J. J. Thomson, *Rights, Restitution, and Risk* (Cambridge, MA: Harvard University Press, 1986), p. 40, defines a violation as an unjust infringement.
11 Cf. Shapiro, *The Evolution of Rights*, pp. 118–20.
12 See R. Polin, 'The Rights of Man in Hobbes and Locke' in Raphael, ed., *Political Theory*, p. 21.
13 J. Locke, *Two Treatises of Government*, ed. P. Laslett (New York: Mentor Books, New American Library, 1963), 'Second Treatise', para. 6.
14 Ibid., para. 57.
15 Ibid., paras 25, 61, 149.
16 Cf. C. B. Macpherson, *The Political Theory of Possessive Individualism* (Oxford: Oxford University Press, 1962); Shapiro, *The Evolution of Rights*, pp. 137–48.
17 Ibid., pp. 127–8 versus G. Parry, *John Locke* (London: Allen and Unwin, 1978), p. 42.
18 Locke, 'Second Treatise', para. 95.
19 E. Burke, *Reflections on the Revolution in France*, ed. C. C. O'Brien (Harmondsworth: Penguin, 1969), p. 119.
20 Ibid., pp. 149–51, 153, 194–5.
21 T. Paine, *Rights of Man* (Harmondsworth: Penguin, 1969), pp. 88, 90, 166.
22 See M. Philp, *Paine* (Oxford: Oxford University Press, 1989).

23 B. Parekh, ed., *Bentham's Political Thought* (London: Croom Helm, 1973), p. 269.

24 R. Harrison, *Bentham* (London: Routledge and Kegan Paul, 1983), pp. 82–3.

25 Quoted in J. Waldron, *Nonsense upon Stilts: Bentham, Burke and Marx on the Rights of Man* (London: Methuen, 1987), p. 69.

26 See D. Lyons, 'Rights, Claimants, and Beneficiaries', *American Philosophical Quarterly*, Vol. 6 (1969), pp. 173–85 for some qualifications to that rule.

27 Parekh, *Bentham's Political Thought* (London: Croom Helm, 1973), pp. 175–94.

28 See ibid., pp. 188–9 and H. L. A. Hart, *Essays on Bentham* (Oxford: Oxford University Press, 1982), Chapter 7. For further discussion see Chapter 4 below.

29 See H. L. A. Hart, *Essays on Bentham* (Oxford: Oxford University Press, 1982), p. 83.

30 Quoted in Waldron, *Nonsense upon Stilts*, pp. 72, 75.

31 See Chapter 5 on Ritchie.

32 T. H. Green, *Lectures on the Principles of Political Obligation* (London: Longmans, 1941: first published 1886), p. 67. See also M. Richter, *The Politics of Conscience: T. H. Green and his Age* (London: Weidenfeld and Nicolson, 1964), especially Chapter 8.

33 Green, *Lectures*, pp. 34, 44–5, 47, 113.

34 Ibid., pp. 37–41, 143, 144, 155–6, 159.

35 Ibid., p. 110.

36 K. Marx, 'On the Jewish Question' in Karl Marx, *Selected Writings* (ed. D. McLellan) (Oxford: Oxford University Press, 1977), pp. 52–3.

37 K. Marx, *Capital*, Vol. 1 (excerpt in *Selected Writings*, p. 455).

38 K. Marx, 'Critique of the Gotha Programme', *Selected Writings*, pp. 568–9. See also S. Lukes, *Marxism and Morality* (Oxford: Oxford University Press, 1985), pp. 27–70.

39 K. Marx, 'On the Jewish Question', pp. 51, 44, 54. See also Waldron, *Nonsense upon Stilts*, p. 132.

Chapter 3

1 See Chapter 1.

2 See e.g. The American Declaration of Independence.

3 Finnis, *Natural Law and Natural Rights*, pp. 205–10.

4 R. Dworkin, *Taking Rights Seriously* (London: Duckworth, 1977), p. 171.

5 J. Raz, *The Morality of Freedom* (Oxford: Oxford University Press, 1986), pp. 193–216.

6 L. W. Sumner, *The Moral Foundation of Rights* (Oxford: Oxford University Press, 1989), pp. 104–5, 151.

7 J. Griffin, *Well-Being* (Oxford: Oxford University Press, 1986), p. 238. Emphasis in the original.

8 Dworkin, *Taking Rights Seriously*, p. xi.

9 H. J. McCloskey, 'Respect for Human Moral Rights versus Maximizing Good', in Frey, *Utility and Rights*, pp. 127–8.

10 Finnis, *Natural Law and Natural Rights*, pp. 64–9.

11 On the need to relate moral rights arguments to empirical evidence see D. Lyons, 'Human Rights and the General Welfare', *Philosophy and Public Affairs*, Vol. 6 (1977), p. 129.

12 MacCormick, *Legal Right and Social Democracy*, p. 129.

13 See the section below on equality.

14 Nickel, *Making Sense of Human Rights*, p. 82. See also K. Baier, 'When does the Right to Life Begin?' in Pennock and Chapman, eds, *Human Rights*, p. 214.

15 Gewirth, 'A Reply to Danto', p. 34.

16 See Golding, 'Towards a Theory of Human Rights', pp. 532–3.

17 C. Taylor, 'Human Rights: The Legal Culture' in *Philosophical Foundations of Human Rights* (Paris: UNESCO, 1986), p. 50.

18 L. Lomasky, 'Personal Projects as the Foundation for Basic Rights', *Social Philosophy and Policy*, Vol. 1 (1984), p. 36. For a further discussion of trade offs see Chapter 6.

19 H. L. A. Hart, 'Are There Any Natural Rights?', *Philosophical Review*, Vol. 64 (1955), pp. 183–7; W. N. Nelson, 'Special Rights, General Rights, and Social Justice', *Philosophy and Public Affairs*, Vol. 3 (1974), pp. 411–13. For a discussion of self-assumed obligations that give rise to rights see R. E. Goodin, *Protecting the Vulnerable* (Chicago: University of Chicago Press, 1985), Chapter 3.

20 R. Tuck, 'The International Bill of Rights', *Philosophical Foundations of Human Rights* (Paris: UNESCO, 1986), p. 74.

21 See T. Campbell, 'The Rights of the Mentally Ill' in Campbell et al., eds, *Human Rights: From Rhetoric to Reality* (Oxford: Blackwell, 1986), pp. 144–5. See also Chapters 4 and 5 below.

22 For a good discussion of these terms see Feinberg, *Rights, Justice and the Bounds of Liberty*, pp. 238–42.

23 Locke's labour theory of property bears that interpretation. See L. C. Becker, *Property Rights* (London: Routledge and Kegan Paul, 1977), pp. 48–56.

24 See M. Freeden, 'Rights, Needs and Community: The Emergence of British Welfare Thought' in R. E. Goodin and A. Ware, eds, *Needs and Welfare* (London: Sage Publications, 1990).

25 M. Cranston, 'Human Rights, Real and Supposed' in Raphael, *Political Theory and the Rights of Man*, p. 50.

26 This is further discussed in the next chapter. For an elaboration of these issues, see Thomson, *Rights, Restitution, and Risk*, Chapter 1.

27 Contrast Golding, 'Towards a Theory of Human Rights', p. 548 with G. Vlastos, 'Justice and Equality' in J. Waldron, ed., *Theories of Rights* (Oxford: Oxford University Press, 1984), p. 47.

28 McCloskey, 'Respect for Human Moral Rights', p. 132.

29 On this point see J. Feinberg, *Social Philosophy* (Englewood Cliffs, NJ: Prentice-Hall, 1973), p. 97.

30 See A. J. M. Milne, *Human Rights and Human Diversity* (London: Macmillan, 1986).

31 See Vlastos, 'Justice and Equality', p. 55.

32 See R. M. Hare, 'Rights, Utility, and Universalization: Reply to J. L. Mackie', in Frey, *Utility and Rights*, pp. 111, 113, 118.

33 Griffin, *Well-Being*, p. 231.

34 See A. Gewirth, *Human Rights* (Chicago: University of Chicago Press, 1982), pp. 1–5.

35 E.g. Milne, *Human Rights and Human Diversity*.

36 See e.g. M. Lazreq, 'Human Rights, State and Ideology: An Historical Perspective' in A. Pollis and P. Schwab, eds, *Human Rights: Cultural and Ideological Perspectives* (New York: Praeger, 1979), pp. 32–4.

37 A. Pollis and P. Schwab, 'Human Rights: A Western Construct with Limited Applicability', in ibid., p. 14. See also below, Chapter 7.

38 P. Ricoeur, introduction to *Philosophical Foundations of Human Rights*, pp. 16, 26.

Chapter 4

1 For the sake of brevity, I will use choice-rights to include autonomy-rights. But see below for possible tensions between the two.

2 See R. Flathman, *The Practice of Rights* (Cambridge: Cambridge University Press, 1976), pp. 72–3, 100.

3 Hart, 'Are There Any Natural Rights?', pp. 175–91.

4 Gewirth, *Human Rights*, pp. 1–38.

5 Rawls, *A Theory of Justice*, pp. 61, 195–201, 313. For an interpretation of Rawls's position see R. Martin, *Rawls and Rights* (Lawrence, Kansas: University Press of Kansas, 1985) and Shapiro, *The Evolution of Rights in Liberal Theory*, pp. 204–70.

6 I have developed this argument in M. Freeden, 'Human Rights and Welfare: A Communitarian View', *Ethics*, Vol. 100 (1990).

7 See Golding, 'Towards a Theory of Human Rights', p. 541. As Campbell (*The Left and Rights*, p. 89) has put it, 'the power theory is still in the shadow of the contract theory.'

8 Hart, *Essays on Bentham*, pp. 162–93.

9 R. Tuck, *Natural Rights Theories: Their Origins and Development* (Cambridge: Cambridge University Press, 1979), pp. 25–7, shows that the mediaeval thinker Jean Gerson already defined a right as a dispositional power (or ability) but one that emanated from man being left to his own nature.

10 Campbell, *The Left and Rights*, p. 87.

11 Hart, *Essays on Bentham*, p. 185.

12 Campbell, *The Left and Rights*, p. 290.

13 Golding, 'The Concept of Rights', pp. 44–5.

14 T. M. Scanlon, 'Rights, Goals and Fairness' in Waldron, *Theories of Rights*, p. 147.

15 Tuck, *Natural Rights Theories*, pp. 130–1, 143.

16 Hart, *Essays on Bentham*, pp. 189–91.

17 See above Chapter 2 and Finnis, *Natural Law*, pp. 204–5.

18 See also Lyons, 'Rights, Claimants, and Beneficiaries', p. 175.

19 Ibid., p. 176, and S. Stoljar, *An Analysis of Rights* (London: Macmillan, 1984), pp. 25–35.

20 Feinberg, *Rights, Justice and the Bounds of Liberty*, pp. 241–2, 216, 249.

21 See MacCormick, *Legal Right and Social Democracy*, p. 160.

22 See also Stoljar, *An Analysis of Rights*, p. 31. Not every interest justifies protection by a right. See R. B. Brandt, 'The Concept of a Moral Right and its Function', *Journal of Philosophy*, Vol. 80 (1983), p. 44.

23 Feinberg, *Rights, Justice and the Bounds of Liberty*, p. 177.

24 C. Wellman, *Welfare Rights* (Totowa, NJ: Rowman and Allanheld, 1982), pp. 24–6.

25 Ibid., p. 197.

26 See Becker, *Property Rights*.

27 R. Nozick's *Anarchy, State, and Utopia* (Oxford: Blackwell, 1974), offers an extreme version of the right of individuals to own their capacities and their existing possessions or those obtained under market consensual conditions. See also Shapiro, *The Evolution of Rights*, pp. 155–203.

28 Golding, 'Towards a Theory of Human Rights', p. 542.

29 See R. Plant, 'Needs, Agency, and Welfare Rights' in J. D. Moon, *Responsibility, Rights and Welfare* (Boulder, CO: Westview, 1988), pp. 60–1.

30 See also M. P. Golding, 'The Primacy of Welfare Rights', *Social Philosophy and Policy*, Vol. 1, (1984), pp. 135–6.

31 Tuck (*Natural Rights Theories*, pp. 50, 53, and Chapter 3), terming welfare-rights objective and liberty/choice-rights subjective and active, finds an early example of their differentiation in Grotius's writings.

32 As Sumner (*The Moral Foundation of Rights*, p. 97), suggests.

33 For a critique of the paternalism of the welfare state see H. J. McCloskey, 'The Moralism and Paternalism Inherent in Enforcing Respect for Human Rights' in C. Sampford and D. J. Galligan, eds, *Law, Rights and the Welfare State* (London: Croom Helm, 1986).

34 L. E. Lomasky, *Persons, Rights, and the Moral Community* (New York: Oxford University Press, 1987), pp. 94–100.

35 MacCormick, *Legal Right*, p. 165.

36 Plant, 'Needs, Agency, and Welfare Rights', p. 68.

37 C. Fried, *Right and Wrong* (Cambridge, MA: Harvard University Press, 1978), p. 154.

38 Ibid., p. 112.

39 Ibid., pp. 120–7.

40 As does Lomasky in *Persons, Rights and the Moral Community*, pp. 39, 52.

41 Lomasky, 'Personal Projects as the Foundation for Basic Rights', p. 41. Unlike Fried, Lomasky is prepared to consider overriding a liberty-right when the ability of individuals to pursue their own projects is in question (p. 54).

42 But not Sumner, *The Moral Foundation of Rights*, p. 206.

43 See Hart, 'Are There Any Natural Rights?'

44 In the case of children; see MacCormick, *Legal Right*, p. 159.

45 See also S. M. Okin, 'Liberty and Welfare: Some Issues in Human Rights Theory' in Pennock and Chapman, *Human Rights*, pp. 230–56.

46 Feinberg, *Rights, Justice and the Bounds of Liberty*, p. 208.

47 Although arguably birth is the initiation of social membership and the rights deriving from that status; see Chapter 5.

48 See e.g. Hart, 'Are There Any Natural Rights?', p. 181.

Chapter 5

1 See I. Berlin, 'The Originality of Machiavelli' in I. Berlin, *Against the Current* (London: The Hogarth Press, 1979), pp. 25–79.

2 J. S. Mill, *On Liberty* (London: J. W. Parker and Son, 1859) may be read in that light.

3 D. G. Ritchie, *Natural Rights* (London: Allen and Unwin, 1952), lst edn 1894, p. 98.

4 Feinberg, *Rights, Justice and the Bounds of Liberty*, pp. 165, 170.

5 Griffin, *Well-Being*, p. 226.

6 Fried, *Right and Wrong*, p. 124.

7 To complicate matters further there is an important sense in which a want may transform itself into a psychological need, however pathological. Whether it is better to satisfy it, or to eliminate the want, is a question both for moralists and psychologists. See also Chapter 4.

8 See e.g. Sumner, *The Moral Foundation of Rights*, pp. 125–6.

9 The ranking of fundamental and derivative rights is another matter, and will receive consideration below.

10 L. Gostin, 'Towards Resolving the Conflict', in L. Gostin, ed., *Civil Liberties in Conflict* (London: Routledge, 1988), p. 8.

11 Ibid.

12 J. Dunn, 'Rights and Political Conflict', in Gostin, *Civil Liberties*, p. 30. See also Raz, *The Morality of Freedom*, pp. 202 ff.

13 See my 'Human Rights and Welfare: A Communitarian View'.

14 L. T. Hobhouse, *Liberalism* (London: Williams and Norgate, 1911), p. 124.

15 See Chapter 4.

16 Feinberg, *Rights, Justice and the Bounds of Liberty*, pp. 233, 247.

17 D. D. Raphael, 'Human Rights, Old and New', in Raphael, ed., *Political Theory and the Rights of Man*, p. 56.

18 This is even accepted by Fried, *Right and Wrong*, p. 112.

19 D. Harris, *Justifying State Welfare* (Oxford: Blackwell, 1987), p. 163.

20 Milne, *Human Rights and Human Diversity*, p. 39.

21 For a useful discussion see ibid., pp. 39–41.

22 M. Sandel, *Liberalism and the Limits of Justice* (Cambridge: Cambridge University Press, 1982), pp. 147–65, 174, 182.

23 J. Humphrey, 'The International Bill of Rights', *Philosophical Foundations of Human Rights* (Paris: UNESCO), p. 62.

24 Tuck, *Natural Rights Theories*, p. 150.

25 Ibid., pp. 56, 68.

26 Ritchie, *Natural Rights*, p. 87. For a further discussion of these issues see Freeden, 'Rights, Needs and Community'.

27 Ritchie, *Natural Rights*, p. 98.

28 D. G. Ritchie, *Darwin and Hegel* (London: Swan Sonnenschein and Co., 1893), pp. 62–3; *Natural Rights*, pp. 101, 103. See also M. Freeden, *The New Liberalism: An Ideology of Social Reform* (Oxford: Oxford University Press, 1978), pp. 97–9.

29 J. A. Hobson, *The Social Problem* (London: J. Nisbet and Co., 1901), p. 150.

30 L. T. Hobhouse, 'The Historical Evolution of Property, in Fact and in Idea' in C. Gore, ed., *Property. Its Duties and Rights* (London: Macmillan and Co., 1913), p. 31. See also L. T. Hobhouse, *The Elements of Social Justice* (London: Allen and Unwin, 1922), pp. 95–9 and M. Freeden, *Liberalism Divided: A Study in British Political Thought 1914–1939* (Oxford: Oxford University Press, 1986), Chapter 7.

31 Hobson, *The Social Problem*, pp. 148–9.

32 On the latter see J. Crawford, ed., *The Rights of Peoples* (Oxford: Oxford University Press, 1988). P. Sieghart, however, objects to using the term 'human rights' to refer to the rights of peoples as separate

entities *The Lawful Rights of Mankind* (Oxford: Oxford University Press, 1986) pp. 161–8.

33 Raz, *The Morality of Freedom*, pp. 207–9.

34 C. Taylor, 'Human Rights: The Legal Culture' in *Philosophical Foundations of Human Rights*, pp. 55–6.

35 See Chapter 3 on alienation.

36 Feinberg, 'The Nature and Value of Rights', p. 244.

37 Tuck, *Natural Rights Theories*, p. 6. Others argue the same in terms of needs, which are of course shared with animals (see R. J. Vincent, *Human Rights and International Relations* (Cambridge: Cambridge University Press, 1986), p. 2).

38 D. Lyons, 'The Correlativity of Rights and Duties', *Nous*, Vol. 4 (1970), p. 46.

39 McCloskey, 'Respect for Human Moral Rights', p. 123.

40 White, *Rights*, pp. 55–73.

41 See Stoljar, *An Analysis of Rights*, p. 55.

42 See Flathman, *The Practice of Rights*, pp. 38–9.

43 Baier, 'When does the Right to Life Begin?', p. 206.

44 See Chapter 1 and Raz, *The Morality of Freedom*, pp. 170–1.

45 Cf. McCloskey, 'Respect for Human Moral Rights', p. 122, and R. Martin and J. W. Nickel, 'Recent Work on the Concept of Rights', *American Philosophical Quarterly*, Vol. 17 (1980), p. 167.

46 Stoljar, *An Analysis of Rights*, Chapter 4, provides a good discussion of the correlativity problem.

47 J. Narveson, 'Contractarian Rights', in Frey, *Utility and Rights*, pp. 164–5.

48 White, *Rights*, p. 64.

49 See G. Marshall, 'Rights, Options, and Entitlements' in A. W. B. Simpson, ed., *Oxford Essays in Jurisprudence*, Second Series (Oxford: Oxford University Press, 1973), p. 237.

50 International law now recognizes the juridical personality not only of states but of individuals. See J. P. Humphrey, 'The Magna Carta of Mankind', in P. Davies, ed., *Human Rights* (London: Routledge, 1988), p. 31.

51 See Freeden, 'Rights, Needs and Community'.

Chapter 6

1 Nozick, *Anarchy, State, and Utopia*, pp. 29–33. See e.g. J. Gray, 'John Stuart Mill on Liberty, Utility, and Rights' in Pennock and Chapman, eds, *Human Rights*, pp. 83–4.

2 See V. Held, *Rights and Goods* (Chicago: University of Chicago Press, 1989), pp. 15–17.

3 See also H. L. A. Hart, 'Between Utility and Rights', in A. Ryan, ed., *The Idea of Freedom* (Oxford: Oxford University Press, 1979), p. 77.

4 Dworkin, *Taking Rights Seriously*, pp. 172, 232.

5 D. Lyons, 'Utility and Rights' in Waldron, ed., *Theories of Rights*, p. 126.

6 Dworkin, 'Rights as Trumps', in Waldron, *Theories of Rights*, p. 158.

7 Nozick, *Anarchy, State and Utopia*, pp. 32–3.

8 For this important distinction see Hart's valuable discussion in 'Between Utility and Rights', pp. 77–98.

9 See Held, *Rights and Goods*, pp. 15ff.

10 Cf. Gray, 'John Stuart Mill on Liberty, Utility, and Rights', p. 83.

11 Dworkin, 'Rights as Trumps', p. 158.

12 Dworkin, *Taking Rights Seriously*, p. 269. Cf. J. R. Pennock, 'Rights, Natural Rights, and Human Rights – A General View' in Pennock and Chapman, eds, *Human Rights*, p. 5.

13 Dworkin, *Taking Rights Seriously*, pp. 275–6.

14 See P. Jones, 'Re-Examining Rights', *British Journal of Political Science*, Vol. 19 (1989), p. 84.

15 R. G. Frey, 'Introduction: Utilitarianism and Persons' in Frey, *Utility and Rights*, pp. 3–4, 8.

16 Lyons, 'Utility and Rights', p. 114.

17 Hart, 'Between Utility and Rights', p. 98.

18 Frey, 'Introduction: Utilitarianism and Persons', p. 16.

19 Frey seems ultimately to conclude that the historical contingencies that mould dispositions become internalized ('Act-Utilitarianism, Consequentialism and Moral Rights', in Frey, p. 82). This introduces 'an unthinking motive for action' (p. 84) which most philosophers find anathema but which social theorists must take into account.

20 For problems related to this philosophical concern see Griffin, *Well-Being*, pp. 230–2.

21 Frey, 'Introduction', pp. 9, 15.

22 See Hare's defence of this view as part of a utilitarian perspective in 'Rights, Utility, and Universalization: Reply to J. L. Mackie' in Frey, *Utility and Rights*, p. 110.

23 This relates to the optimization criteria discussed below.

24 Frey, 'Introduction', p. 18.

25 Scanlon, 'Rights, Goals, and Fairness', p. 138. See also Sumner, *The Moral Foundation of Rights*, Chapter 6.

26 J. S. Mill moved a considerable way towards this modified utilitarianism when writing in *On Liberty* of the 'permanent interests of a progressive being', p. 24.

27 This certainly was Bentham's position.

28 Frey, 'Introduction', p. 5.

29 Compare Finnis, *Natural Law and Natural Rights*, especially pp. 118–19 who, while opposed to all types of consequentialism, rightly identifies

the absence of this feature as one of its main difficulties. I argue that those difficulties are surmountable without entirely discarding a utilitarian perspective (although not without taking issue with Finnis's essentialist viewpoint).

30 Steiner takes a more stringent view of the optimal relationship within a set of rights as one in which it is logically impossible for the exercise of one right to interfere with the exercise of another. However, this would restrict rights solely to exclusive individual titles to objects (H. Steiner, 'The Structure of a Set of Compossible Rights' *Journal of Philosophy*, Vol. 74 (1977), pp. 767–75).

31 See above, Chapter 1.

32 Griffin, *Well-Being*, p. 243.

33 Frey, 'Act-Utilitarianism, Consequentialism, and Moral Rights', in Frey, pp. 64–6.

34 Cf. Pennock, 'Rights, Natural Rights, and Human Rights', p. 14.

35 See Chapter 4.

36 This is also related to Feinberg's distinction between a right and the thing to which one has the right, in *Rights, Justice and the Bounds of Liberty*, pp. 242–5.

37 For the latter view see Scanlon, 'Rights, Goals, and Fairness', p. 147.

38 Campbell, *The Left and Rights*, p. 140.

39 An exception has been noted in Chapter 4, when an individual may waive an intolerably costly right to life.

40 Thus Gray, 'John Stuart Mill on Liberty, Utility, and Rights', p. 95, interpreting Mill's prioritizing of liberty over utility. See also J. Gray, 'Indirect Utility and Fundamental Rights', *Social Philosophy and Policy*, Vol. 1 (1984), pp. 73–91.

41 See also A. Gibbard, 'Utilitarianism and Human Rights', *Social Philosophy and Policy*, Vol. 1 (1984), p. 99.

42 Frey, 'Introduction', p. 9.

43 See Waldron, *Theories of Rights*, p. 13.

44 As does Dworkin, *Taking Rights Seriously*, p. xii.

45 This is not to suggest that all societies would invariably benefit from the promulgation and implementation of a rights-theory, but that typically they would.

46 J. L. Mackie, 'Rights, Utility, and Universalization', in Frey, ed., *Utility and Rights*, pp. 89, 100.

47 McCloskey, 'Respect for Human Moral Rights', p. 132.

48 See Lyons, 'Utility and Rights', p. 114.

Chapter 7

1 D. Weissbrodt, 'Human Rights: An Historical Perspective' in Davies, *Human Rights*, p. 1.

2 Sieghart, *The Lawful Rights of Mankind*, p. 83.

3 Nickel, *Making Sense of Human Rights*, pp. 131–46.

4 Contrast CPR, article 2.2 with the International Covenant on Economic, Social and Cultural Rights, article 2.1.

5 For an attempt to adumbrate a sharp core approach, and its ensuing difficulties see E. Oröcö, 'The Core of Rights and Freedoms: The Limit of Limits' in Campbell et al., eds, *Human Rights: From Rhetoric to Reality*, pp. 37–59.

6 For a detailed examination of contemporary rights documents see L. J. Macfarlane, *The Theory and Practice of Human Rights* (Hounslow: Temple Smith, 1985).

7 J. Häusermann, 'Myths and Realities', in Davies, ed., *Human Rights*, p. 144.

8 See L. Levin, 'The Rights of the Child', in Davies, ed., *Human Rights*, p. 48.

9 See Freeden, 'Rights, Needs and Community'.

10 See J. R. Pennock and J. W. Chapman, *Nomos XII: Political and Legal Obligation* (New York: Atherton, 1970).

11 Lord Scarman, foreword to Gostin, *Civil Liberties in Conflict*, p. xiii.

12 Sieghart, *The Lawful Rights of Mankind*, p. 25.

13 See J. Murdoch, 'The Rights of Public Assembly and Procession' in Campbell et al., p. 179, and D. Galligan, 'Preserving Public Protest: The Legal Approach', in Gostin, ed., *Civil Liberties in Conflict*, pp. 42–3.

14 *New York Times* Co. v. United States, 403 US 713 (1971).

15 See Chapter 3 above for a discussion of specific rights.

16 There are, of course, other reasons for ensuring optimal conditions for giving birth and rearing the young, unrelated to the rights of women.

17 See N. Burrows, 'International Law and Human Rights: the Case of Women's Rights', in Campbell et al., eds, p. 85.

18 See N. Dorsen, 'Is There a Right to Stop Offensive Speech? The Case of the Nazis at Skokie', in Gostin, ed., *Civil Liberties in Conflict*, p. 124; and S. Sedley, 'The Spider and the Fly: A Question of Principle', in Gostin, ed., *Civil Liberties in Conflict*, pp. 140–4.

19 Regents of the University of California v. Bakke, 438 US 265 (1978).

20 See A. Diemer, 'The 1948 Declaration: An Analysis of Meanings' in *Philosophical Foundations of Human Rights* (Paris: UNESCO), pp. 95–111.

21 See e.g. Crawford, *The Rights of Peoples*.

22 Mackie, 'Rights, Utility, and Universalization', p. 88.

Select Bibliography

Bandman, E. L. and B., eds, *Bioethics and Human Rights* (Boston: Little, Brown, 1978).

Becker, L. C., *Property Rights* (London: Routledge and Kegan Paul, 1977).

Brandt, R. B., 'The Concept of a Moral Right and its Function', *Journal of Philosophy*, Vol. 80 (1983).

Burke, E., *Reflections on the Revolution in France* (Harmondsworth: Penguin, 1969).

Campbell, T., *The Left and Rights* (London: Routledge and Kegan Paul, 1983).

Campbell, T. et al., eds, *Human Rights: From Rhetoric to Reality* (Oxford: Blackwell, 1986).

Claeys, G., 'The French Revolution Debate and British Political Thought', *History of Political Thought*, Vol. 11 (1990).

Crawford, J., ed., *The Rights of Peoples* (Oxford: Oxford University Press, 1988).

Davies, P., ed., *Human Rights* (London: Routledge, 1988).

Donnelly, J., *The Concept of Human Rights* (London: Croom Helm, 1985).

Dworkin, R., *Taking Rights Seriously* (London: Duckworth, 1977).

Feinberg, J., 'The Nature and Value of Rights', *Journal of Value Inquiry*, Vol. 4 (1970).

Feinberg, J., *Rights, Justice and the Bounds of Liberty* (Princeton: Princeton University Press, 1980).

Feinberg, J., *Social Philosophy* (Englewood Cliffs, NJ: Prentice-Hall, 1973).

Finnis, J., *Natural Law and Natural Rights* (Oxford: Oxford University Press, 1980).

Flathman, R. E., *The Practice of Rights* (Cambridge: Cambridge University Press, 1976).

Frankena, W. K., 'Natural and Inalienable Rights', *Philosophical Review*, Vol. 64 (1955).

Freeden, M., *The New Liberalism: An Ideology of Social Reform* (Oxford: Oxford University Press, 1978).

Freeden, M., *Liberalism Divided: A Study in British Political Thought 1914–1939* (Oxford: Oxford University Press, 1986).

Freeden, M., 'Human Rights and Welfare: A Communitarian View', *Ethics*, Vol. 100 (1990).

Freeden, M., 'Rights, Needs and Community: The Emergence of British Welfare Thought' in R. E. Goodin and A. Ware, eds, *Needs and Welfare* (London: Sage Publications, 1990).

Frey, R. G., ed., *Utility and Rights* (Oxford: Blackwell, 1985).

Fried, C., *Right and Wrong* (Cambridge, MA: Harvard University Press, 1978).

Gallie, W., 'Essentially Contested Concepts', *Proceedings of the Aristotelian Society* (1955–6).

Gewirth, A., *Human Rights* (Chicago: University of Chicago Press, 1982).

Golding, M. P., 'Towards a Theory of Human Rights', *Monist*, Vol. 52 (1968).

Golding, M. P., 'The Concept of Rights: A Historical Sketch' in E. L. Bandman and B. Bandman, *Bioethics and Human Rights* (Boston: Little, Brown, 1978).

Golding, M. P., 'The Primacy of Welfare Rights', *Social Philosophy and Policy*, Vol. 1 (1984).

Goodin, R. E., *Protecting the Vulnerable* (Chicago: University of Chicago Press, 1985).

Gostin, L., ed., *Civil Liberties in Conflict* (London: Routledge, 1988).

Green, T. H., *Lectures on the Principles of Political Obligation* (London: Longmans, 1941).

Griffin, J., *Well-Being* (Oxford: Oxford University Press, 1986).

Harris, D., *Justifying State Welfare* (Oxford: Blackwell, 1987).

Harrison, R., *Bentham* (London: Routledge and Kegan Paul, 1983).

Hart, H. L. A., 'Are There any Natural Rights?', *Philosophical Review*, Vol. 64 (1955).

Hart, H. L. A., 'Between Utility and Rights' in A. Ryan, ed., *The Idea of Freedom* (Oxford: Oxford University Press, 1979).

Hart, H. L. A., *Essays on Bentham* (Oxford: Oxford University Press, 1982).

Held, V., *Rights and Goods* (Chicago: University of Chicago Press, 1989).

Hobbes, T., *Leviathan* (Harmondsworth: Penguin, 1968).

Hobhouse, L. T., *Liberalism* (London: Williams and Norgate, 1911).

Hobhouse, L. T., 'The Historical Evolution of Property, in Fact and in Idea' in C. Gore, ed., *Property, Its Duties and Rights* (London: Macmillan and Co., 1913).

Hobhouse, L. T., *The Elements of Social Justice* (London: Allen and Unwin, 1921).

Hobson, J. A., *The Social Problem* (London: J. Nisbet and Co., 1901).

Hohfeld, W. N., *Fundamental Legal Conceptions* (New Haven: Yale University Press, 1919).

Jones, P., 'Re-Examining Rights', *British Journal of Political Science*, Vol. 19 (1989).

Kamenka, E. and Tay, A. E.-S., eds, *Human Rights* (London: Edward Arnold, 1978).

Locke, J., *Two Treatises of Government* (New York: Mentor Books, New American Library, 1963).

Lomasky, L. E., *Persons, Rights, and the Moral Community* (New York: Oxford University Press, 1987).

Lukes, S., *Marxism and Morality* (Oxford: Oxford University Press, 1985).

Lyons, D., 'Human Rights and the General Welfare', *Philosophy and Public Affairs*, Vol. 6 (1977).

Lyons, D., 'Rights, Claimants, and Beneficiaries', *American Philosophical Review*, Vol. 6 (1969).

Lyons, D., 'The Correlativity of Rights and Duties', *Nous*, Vol. 4 (1970).

MacCormick, N., *Legal Right and Social Democracy* (Oxford: Oxford University Press, 1982).

Macfarlane, L. J., *The Theory and Practice of Human Rights* (Hounslow: Temple Smith, 1985).

Marshall, G., 'Rights, Options, and Entitlements', in A. W. B. Simpson, ed., *Oxford Essays in Jurisprudence*, Second Series (Oxford: Oxford University Press, 1973).

Martin, R., *Rawls and Rights* (Lawrence, Kansas: University Press of Kansas, 1985).

Martin, R. and J. W. Nickel, 'Recent Work on the Concept of Rights', *American Philosophical Quarterly*, Vol. 17 (1980).

Marx, K., *Selected Writing* (ed. D. McLellan) (Oxford: Oxford University Press, 1977).

McCloskey, H. J., 'Rights – Some Conceptual Issues', *Australasian Journal of Philosophy*, Vol. 54 (1976).

Melden, A. I., *Rights and Right Conduct* (Oxford: Basil Blackwell, 1959).

Mill, J. S., *On Liberty* (London: J. W. Parker and Son, 1859).

Milne, A. J. M., *Human Rights and Human Diversity* (London: Macmillan, 1986).

Moon, J. D., ed., *Responsibility, Rights and Welfare* (Boulder, CO: Westview, 1988).

Nelson, W. N., 'Special Rights, General Rights, and Social Justice', *Philosophy and Public Affairs*, Vol. 3 (1974).

Nickel, J. W., *Making Sense of Human Rights* (Berkeley and Los Angeles: University of California Press, 1987).

Nozick, R., *Anarchy, State, and Utopia* (Oxford: Blackwell, 1974).

Paine, T., *Rights of Man* (Harmondsworth: Penguin, 1969).

Parekh, B., ed., *Bentham's Political Thought* (London: Croom Helm, 1973).

Parry, G., *John Locke* (London: Allen and Unwin, 1978).

Pennock, J. R. and J. W. Chapman, eds, *Nomos XXIII: Human Rights* (New York: New York University Press, 1981).

Philosophical Foundations of Human Rights (Paris: UNESCO, 1986).

Philp, M., *Paine* (Oxford: Oxford University Press, 1989).

Plant, R., H. Lesser and P. Taylor-Gooby, *Political Philosophy and Social Welfare* (London: Routledge and Kegan Paul, 1980).

Pollis, A. and P. Schwab, eds, *Human Rights: Cultural and Ideological Perspectives* (New York: Praeger, 1979).

Raphael, D. D., ed., *Political Theory and the Rights of Man* (London: Macmillan, 1967).

Rawls, J., *A Theory of Justice* (Oxford: Oxford University Press, 1972).

Raz, J., *The Morality of Freedom* (Oxford: Oxford University Press, 1986).

Richter, M., *The Politics of Conscience: T. H. Green and His Age* (London: Weidenfeld and Nicolson, 1964).

Ritchie, D. G., *Darwin and Hegel* (London: Swan Sonnenschein and Co., 1893).

Ritchie, D. G., *Natural Rights* (London: Allen and Unwin, 1952).

Sampford, C. J. G. and D. J. Galligan, eds, *Law, Rights and the Welfare State* (London: Croom Helm, 1986).

Sieghart, P., *The Lawful Rights of Mankind* (Oxford: Oxford University Press, 1986).

Shapiro, I., *The Evolution of Rights in Liberal Theory* (Cambridge: Cambridge University Press, 1986).

Social Philosophy and Policy, Vol. 1 (1984) (*Human Rights*).

Steiner, H., 'The Structure of a Set of Compossible Rights', *Journal of Philosophy*, Vol. 74 (1977).

Stoljar, S., *An Analysis of Rights* (London: Macmillan, 1984).

Strauss, L., *Natural Right and History* (Chicago: Chicago University Press, 1953).

Sumner, L. W., *The Moral Foundation of Rights* (Oxford: Oxford University Press, 1989).

Thomson, J. J., *Rights, Restitution, and Risk* (Cambridge, MA: Harvard University Press, 1986).

Thornton, P., *Decade of Decline: Civil Liberties in the Thatcher Years* (London: National Council for Civil Liberties, 1989).

Tuck, R., *Natural Rights Theories: Their Origins and Development* (Cambridge: Cambridge University Press, 1979).

Vincent, R. J., *Human Rights and International Relations* (Cambridge: Cambridge University Press, 1986).

Waldron, J., ed., *Theories of Rights* (Oxford: Oxford University Press, 1984).

Waldron, J., ed., *Nonsense Upon Stilts: Bentham, Burke and Marx on the Rights of Man* (London: Methuen, 1987).

Waldron, J., *The Right to Private Property* (Oxford: Oxford University Press, 1988).

Wellman, C., *Welfare Rights* (Totowa, NJ: Rowman and Allanheld, 1982).

White, A. R., *Rights* (Oxford: Oxford University Press, 1984).

Index